Become Healthier, Wealthier, and Wiser

By Being Aware of

What You Attract

Volume 1

Written and Illustrated

By

Jacob Caldwell

Medical Intuitive - Massage Therapist

©Copyright 2011-2018 by Exoflow, LLC 5429 Russell Ave NW #300, Seattle WA 98107. All rights reserved. No part of this publication may be reproduced by any means or for any reason without the consent of the publisher. The information contained herein is obtained from sources believed to be reliable, but its accuracy cannot be guaranteed.

All material in this publication is provided for information only and may not be construed as medical advice or instruction. No action or inaction should be taken based solely on the contents of this publication: instead, readers should consult appropriate health professionals on any matter relating to their health and well-being. The information and opinions provided in this publication are believed to be accurate and sound, based on the best judgement available to the author, but readers who fail to consult with appropriate health authorities assume the risk of any injuries. The publisher is not responsible for errors or omissions. The material in this report has not been approved by the American Medical Association (AMA) or the FDA. The products and materials discussed are not intended to diagnose, treat, cure, or prevent any disease.

This Book is Dedicated to Pam

Who was (and is) a great friend at the time of when all this information in this book came to me.

She helped me calibrate this information and helped me find the truth in my voice and gave me the courage and confidence to present this material.

...and special thanks...

... to Caroline who helped edit this book. You should have seen it three versions ago. For her to tackle this editing job and make it readable for you was quite a task. For a second, I thought she changed the text color to red, nope, there was just that much that needed to change. Thanks Caroline for helping take my vision and making it readable. I appreciate it a lot and appreciate you!

Contents

Introduction..x

Chapter 1 – Anatomy of the Aura..1

The Chakra..3

What is a Medical Intuitive?..5

The Rainbow Aura..8

The Light Bulb Body...9

The 10 Chakras..11

Male and Female Energy..22

The 3 Connections...28

Thinkers and Doers..32

Chapter 2 – Without One there is None..37

Wooing the Lady Manifestation..40

Chapter 3 – The Too Strong and Too Weak Chakras..........................49

Cause, Affects, and Balance...49

The Aura of Attraction Survey..60

The Too Strong Chakras..66

The Too Weak Chakras..76

Your Attraction Pattern affects all aspects of your Life..........................86

Chapter 4 – Cords, Objects, and Entities...Oh my!.....................89

What are Cords..89

Mental Telepathy..90

Why do we Cord...93

Why do I keep Attracting these Jerks?...99

Attachment and Detachment of Cords...103

Objects..109

Entities..118

Praying..121

Energy Vampires..122

Cord Cutting..124

Afterword – More Books by Jacob Caldwell.............................131

Introduction

The material in this book is compiled and written through the eyes of my experience as a Medical Intuitive. The stories I convey here have been compiled from information gained in those sessions. It has taken me a long time to believe some of my own information as there is little way to affirm that the information gained was from being Intuitive. So, trying to prove my information with science may be a little ahead of its time but perhaps in the future this can be proven. What can be proven within my methods is that people have found peace, symptoms have been resolved, and healings have occurred with people who have previously sought treatment from every other medical modality. The joy and the ah ha moments that have come up from some of the people I have worked with are validation enough for me.

    I believe the message I have in this book is a piece of the equation to discovering why we are here on Earth now and what we came here to do. I believe I have discovered a technique that can explain how we get sick in the spiritual sense and how to resolve it. A lot of what I do is in the invisible and it is tough to prove, but people's eyes tell me that what I see and what I am telling them is the truth.

So, I suggest viewing my story with an open mind as I am sure you will find a piece of yourself multiple times in this book. This book will help you resolve some of the issues you did not know existed and will help you discover that there are solutions for you everywhere if you just look at things in a new way. I believe this book can fit within the subject of how to be a human.

The process of writing this book has helped to heal multiple areas in my life. I started this book over a decade ago. It seems every year I would have to do some personal energy work that involved culminating this information together and getting it out of my head. Throughout my life, I have overcome many personal issues that I have worked very hard to bury and ignore. This book has helped me to divulge and expose many of these issues and to shine a light on my own darkness. Healing can only begin when light exposes the darkness. A big starting point for issues to overcome was when I was diagnosed with a learning disability in grade school. The label was debilitating in and of itself and I held the belief that I was disabled in some way because the teacher said so. It is true that left-brained activities like writing, grammar and comprehension were always difficult for me because I am a very right-brained. So, this idea of writing a book seemed like a monumental task. The subject I am writing about is really "out there" for some people and that was another obstacle I had to overcome, was whether I had the qualifications to write about such a subject. There is some research being done, and others are doing a similar thing, but I believe I am going into areas that are not mainstream, and I could be easily be labeled as a "nutjob". However, I believe strongly that I am adding a piece to the New Age Movement that can assist people in understanding more about what is going on in our rapidly changing world. Plus, in the sessions I have done I have had many thankful people who I have helped, and this is enough evidence for me. I have had too much success for a drive-by naysayer to have any effect on me.

Deciding to do all the illustrations myself has been its own challenge. I would say I am a pretty good conceptual artist but not a fine artist. Tackling the illustrations has been another leap of courage to show off my non-fine art skills. People are going to find some misspellings, possibly some bad grammar and poor illustrating, and frankly I don't care. What I am mostly concerned about is that the concepts in this book help you in your life. Anything less than that, I don't really care about. So, if one wants to disregard my message because I walk on the wrong side of the street or choose bad grammar, then good for you and I have plenty of other mistakes for you to find as well. This book is for the spiritually mature people who want to be responsible for their own life and heal themselves to ascend to the next level. This book is for people who already have done the work on themselves and just need that last little nugget of info to ascend over the peak. If the last two sentences were too stunning for you, then I really suggest putting your judgments aside and thank yourself later that you could finish reading at least a couple of chapters. And if you are able to read this book cover to cover and grasp the concepts in it then we should have lunch sometime because we may have a lot to talk about.

Chapter 1

The Anatomy of the Aura

As long as the New Age Movement has been around, the 7 Chakra Model has been right there with it. Originally from the Hindu religion, it came to America in the early 1900's. It has always been a backdrop and a reference for energy flow throughout the body. Many workshops have been spawned off this information and the rainbow hue that envelops the body has always been an inspiring picture.

Through many of my studies of spiritual and ancient work I have noticed as things get passed down from one generation to the next there will always be information that is missing, to either protect the information itself or to manipulate people with misinformation. I am not certain this has happened to the 7 Chakra rainbow model but through my maturation as a spiritual healer, the model has made very little sense to me.

In 2004 I worked with the Perelandra Flower essences and used the practice of the book that accompanies the work called, the Brotherhood and Sisterhood of Light. They have a nice technique of mediating and downloading information. I had a 6 month download where I channeled mandalas and created a series called the "Stepladder to Enlightenment".

They are a series of mandalas that raised people's frequency in incremental steps.

Through the years of integrating all this additional information, was born the current model of what I use in my Medical Intuitive work today. The information that was downloaded was the complete plan of what I call the 10 Chakra Model. Since is it like the 7 Chakra Model, I do not know if my model is an add-on or another chakra system that is on a separate dimension or density. In Hindu practices of the chakras there are many more categories like Minor and Major chakras and upwards to hundreds of other chakras.

As I continued to put all the pieces together I started to see the 10 Chakra Model as a complete self-contained system with multiple validations. There are multiple ways that the 10 Chakra model would stand up and that it would correspond with the organs of the body and other modalities like Numerology. Further into the Chapter I will illustrate that the 10 Chakra model can be broken into 5 pairs of Male and Female Chakras and the model can be split in half called the "Thinkers and the Doers". It seems this system was not just a random model I have made up. I speculate that the 10 Chakra model is filling in missing information of the 7 Chakras or it is another overlay of the energy body.

The 10 individual chakras are named by what they do. Each has a power name of action or feeling that self describes the energy of that chakra. I believe that is why the 7 Chakra Model is not that helpful as people do not know what to do with the information or the rainbow concept. The 7 Chakra Rainbow model is a nice picture to put on a wall in a healing center, however, it gives no more information after that or how it would be useful to one in their everyday life.

What I would like to display is a more elaborate system that I believe will encourage people to take a deeper look at what one can do with the chakra system and make more sense on how one can involve it in their lives. There have been many "How to Chakra" workshops where they discuss and compartmentalize each chakra and its attributes. With the 10 Chakra Model,

I believe I can not only compartmentalize but show how all 10 works together and how they work in our daily lives through relationships, business, and projects.

The Chakra

The Chakra will be a common term used throughout this book. It has many references likened to an energy vortex. A chakra is a spiral of energy that radiates from the spine outwardly to the outer edge of the Aura. The aura is the outer realm of the light energy from the initial chakra vortex.

To help make sense of a chakra light system, they are broken down into categories much like a rainbow. A rainbow is essentially one light source that then prisms into distinct categories. In a chakra model, each category is labeled with a distinguishing feature that makes up the whole.

The seashell represents a notable example of a 3D energy vortex emulating from a pinpoint source expanding and spiraling out into a larger area. The expansion distance of the spiral energy depends upon the amount of energy initially projected.

No need for Color and Rainbows

Throughout my practice, I have not used a color system of any kind when working with the chakras. If one uses the 7 Chakra Model one can use those colors to see where their talents may already lie and correspond with those chakras. However, this has never come up in sessions as a way of helping people with their issues. The only time I use color is when I do my "party trick", where I can see people's aura color. I can see the first three dominant colors of people's aura. I have found that these dominant colors correspond to a person's favorite color. So, if one chooses colors for a team or for a project and one keeps choosing the same particular color, what one is doing is expressing a part of themselves that they are like. Like attracts like and we usually like the things that are like us. My favorite color is orange and when I was growing up my favorite foods were orange colored which involved oranges, orange soda pop, and I still like sweet and sour orange anything. However, in the 10 Chakra model, color is not going to be mentioned as it is not important, and it has never come up. I thought of possibly adding white, black, and gray to the 7 colors to round up to 10 but then some things wouldn't match up. So now I believe color has nothing to do with this 10 Chakra Model. The most important concept about the 10 chakras system is whether the energy is turned on or off. Having a chakra on or off can have specific consequences to the outcomes of people's lives and this will be one of the main premises of this book.

Validation of Information

I do not have science behind me to help validate what I have learned but have somewhat done that myself and hold myself very accountable. Intentionally tricking people to have them believe me is not my way of doing things and would be very boring and unfulfilling to me. Plus, you can see the truth in someone's eyes when conveying these messages. When I am right on, I can see the glow and excitement in their eyes and I have the same feelings of excitement when I am connecting with them properly.

Hollywood has given the impression that Healers will be quite exhausted from channeling information or assisting with a group healing. This makes things look more dramatic than they are. Sometimes a Healer does become exhausted, but I have observed if this is the case then usually the Healer has a bad technique that is hurting them. In my sessions, I find it very exciting to help someone accomplish a state of healing that they haven't found yet, especially if the client has had many other prior treatments that have not worked for them. A great enlightening session can bring me joy and validation for what I do and afterwards I can be buzzing for days off the success and newly learned breakthroughs.

Sometimes in a session I have assumed and guessed what a symptom may mean or have been a little off and I can see the confusion in their eyes, which means I am incorrect. One may be able to trick and hype someone off the trail, but you can't keep that up for long. I can now recognize this look and start over and then I will get some better information. This is how I discern my own truth and have calibrated these results with how my body feels and the reaction from others.

What motivates and excites me is unveiling something about the person that will empower or inspire their healing. I have conducted my own self tests around validating this system. To this day, it has not let me down. As a Medical Intuitive, in session, I do not need for the person to tell me anything, unless they want to work on something specific, but usually it starts by me asking their Higher Self, "What does this person need to work on next?" I then relay the information to the client which helps validate and focus the information. So, if one has told me nothing and I come up with accurate relevant information after the energy balancing, they will feel better and to them the information is right on, and that is enough validation. Throughout this book, each concept that I bring up has been validated through multiple people. In working with a few people, I can triangulate the commonalities of each issue and then confidently draw some conclusions about everyday common diseases and circumstances that would seem foreign and irrelevant to a Western Medical physician. What I am going to display throughout this book is the information that I have discovered during my Medical Intuitive sessions and have experienced in my own life.

What is a Medical Intuitive?

A Medical Intuitive is a holistic practitioner that can investigate the body like an x-ray and see what and where diseases lie and comprehend how issues manifested. My Medical Intuitive practice is mostly centered on how things work and how things are caused. There are three parts I address in a session:

(1) Identifying what chakras are out of balance and the drama around the event that first initiated the imbalance.
(2) How this imbalance is affecting the person daily in their job, relationships, or projects.
(3) After the imbalance is energetically balanced, then we discuss how to maintain the new balance into the future. Counseling the person to be more aware of how their energy works so in the future they can be more preventative and proactive with their energy and choices, so they do not recreate the initial imbalance.

This has been my focus from the beginning, to empower people on how to heal themselves and be more aware of what they do with their energy.

Whenever I scan a body there will always be an image that will represent what the person's issue is. The image will unfold like a movie and I will watch the person move around in that environment and the whole story of the issue will be revealed. I can see if energy is attacking them or if they are using their energy inefficiently. With this information, I can interpret just about any issue one may be having. By asking the question to the person's Higher Self I can come up with useful information for that person. I can talk to the person while they are in the movie and they will tell me what they are doing. I can see energy that may attack them, and I will ask the energy, "Why are you doing that and what are you doing to that person?" All energy comes from a source and that intention can be tracked, talked to, and once addressed it can be cleared.

As a Medical Intuitive, I feel it is important to empower people through health. Our health and sickness are guides on how to live. Unfortunately, people do not think that they have any power over their health. Every disease and imbalanced issue that I have seen are the result of bad choices that a person has made. Our bodies let us know when our mind is not in a healthy state. When we can consciously connect our health as guidance on how to live, then we will truly know how to live in joy.

I believe that as a Medical Intuitive my role is to help people interpret what their body is saying to them. It seems the real definition of my Medical Intuitive practice is about redefining what the Mind thinks is right and wrong. We get so caught up sometimes with trying to do the "right thing" no matter what the consequences are, even if it may make us ill. We need to see that the illness is telling us that the "right thing" is wrong. Often, our truth is based on appeasing someone or assuming a collective belief is true. Often those people do not know what they are doing, so we literally have the blind leading the blind. If we can listen to a different interpretation and trust what our bodies want to do, then we can truly live a healthy life with confidence and certainty.

Energy is Light, and Light is Energy

One of main topics of this book will be about energy and how it is used. The human body generates massive amounts of energy. Kirlian photography has demonstrated that all physical objects have energy moving through them. The more conductive they are the more energy is apparent in the Kirlian pictures.

Our bones are made up of minerals which fall into the category of metal. Metal is conductive, so our bones can direct energy. Energy can be sourced from the center of the Universe, from the Sun, and our Higher Self. When we connect with these Original Sources we can be fueled with infinite energy.

The source of energy is first received through the crown of the head to the top of the "antennae", the pineal gland, then the spinal column and to the nervous system which distributes energy throughout the body. The nervous system acts a lot like light as it is radiating energy throughout the body. Energy moves through the nervous system like fiber optics. The power and strength of energy that radiates through a person is measured by the health of an individual. If energy moves easily and efficiently through a human body, one will receive true health. If one lets energy stop and becomes stagnant or suppresses energy in their body, this is what dis-ease really is – lack of free flow of energy.

The Rainbow Aura and our Natural Light

The popular 7 Chakra Model has a beautiful rainbow association with it. I agree that the rainbow goes well with the associated colors. It even works the same way with sound frequency. Each color has a sound frequency and the lowest sound is Red. As we go up in frequency we will correspond with the other colors and the highest frequencies are at the top of the rainbow which are White and Pink.

If energy is light, then the rainbow model will not hold. Light moves away from the source in concentric circles, like when a pebble thrown on a pond creates concentric waves. With the wave model, a person's aura will not look like a rainbow in horizontal bars.

We have seen physical natural auras in the world like the Sunbow, Moon bow, and the light around a light bulb. This is what the human aura looks like. The color of a person's aura corresponds to who the person is and their purpose here on Earth.

The more inline one is with their purpose and their zest for life, the brighter one's aura will be. When we are in full bliss this means we are in line with the laws of the universe, and the natural energy that shines through becomes brighter and more recognizable to other people.

On the other hand, dull or dimly lit auras will be just the opposite. If we block our light due to fear or personal disempowerment this will restrict the energy of our aura. These people may turn more to the drama side to try and take the light from others, as these dull light people think they cannot do things themselves.

Since each color corresponds to a chakra or organ this will also dictate what our aura looks like. If one is a good speaker, they may have the color of blue or cyan around them. Green is often associated with healers and people who are compassionate. There are many books on the 7 Chakra colors, so I am not going to go into those details.

The color of your aura may change with the activity that you are doing. If you are playing gentle meditative music your aura will look soft and radiate most of the pastel colors. If you are playing a sport that requires a little more testosterone, one will have jagged intense yellow-orange-red colors. If someone is in high anxiety, their aura will look like a bunch of energetic zig-zaggy lines and it will be difficult to stand next to them.

The Light Bulb Body

The Light Bulb is much like the anatomy of the Chakra system. The main energy is captured in the spinal column just like a filament in a light bulb. The light extends past the bulb into the rest of the room which is also what the human aura does. When someone observes another person walking into a room and "lights it up", they are referring to the amount of energy and vivaciousness that is coming off of that person. The stronger amperage one has, the brighter their aura will be, and it can affect the whole room and groups of people. A positive person can charge up a room just like someone with low amperage can suck the light and life out of a room.
The filament of a light bulb is much like the spinal column in the human body. Chakras have specific points that are spaced out along the spinal column. The Chakra locations will be congruent with the local organs. The organs of the body which have their own individual purpose and will shine with the light that is conducted to them. Each organ has a different purpose and intent, so

the light will shine differently from each organ, hence, the differentiation of specific categories of colors for chakras.

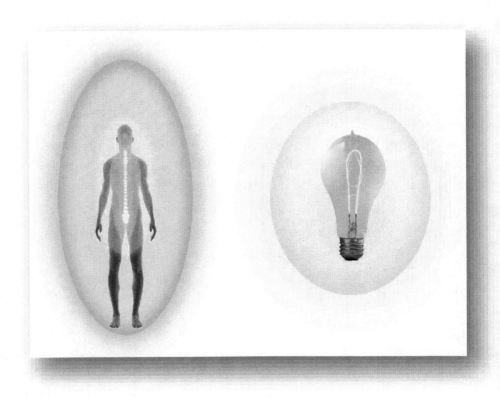

The 10 Chakras

This is a list of chakras by location, function, and their characteristic of balance. The list starts above the top of the head and goes down towards the feet.

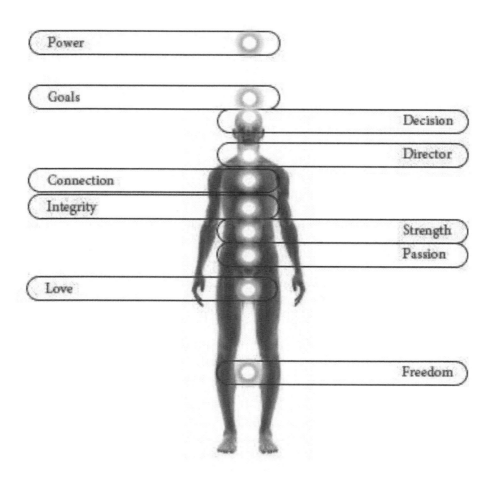

Power Chakra

Feminine

Location: The Feminine Power Chakra is located about a foot and a half from the top of the head. If one does the goddess pose, arms raised above the head, elbows slightly bent with hands coming together to make a circle, one will activate the Power Chakra.

Function:

• The Power Chakra holds all the information of who we are and what we came here to do.

• It is the first Chakra that connects us to the Source of all that "is".

• This Chakra is the first receiver of the Male Energy* (*See The Three Connections).

✦ The Power Chakra represents all things that are ours and which cannot be taken from us like our purpose in life, hair color, body type, and name.

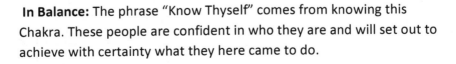

In Balance: The phrase "Know Thyself" comes from knowing this Chakra. These people are confident in who they are and will set out to achieve with certainty what they here came to do.

The Goal Chakra

Feminine

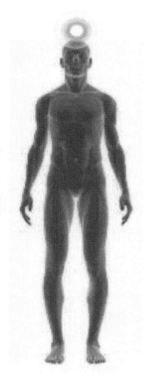

Location: The top of the head controlling the top part of the brain

Function:

• To set the intention of how one wants to feel towards things and situations when they are completed.
In the end, how do you want to feel?

In Balance: When the Goal Chakra is mastered, one will be   able to stay in a constant state of bliss no matter what the circumstance. The Goal Chakra requires being consciously aware of the feelings that one wants to hold at the end of a project. Initiating this intention at the beginning of the day will help affirm and align your day to be of bliss.

Anxiety is a reminder that you have not used your Goal Chakra. Anxiety is an intention that

the Goal will fail.

The Decision Chakra

Masculine

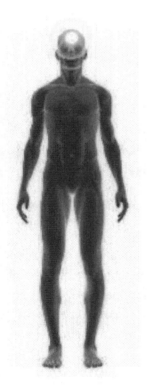

Location: The Masculine Decision Chakra is focused in the bottom half of the brain. It is also thought of as the Chakra of vision, also known as the "Third Eye".

Function:

- How tasks will be implemented.

- The Vision of how the details of plans will come to full manifestation.

In Balance: When this Chakra is in balance, one will lay out the best possible plans for an easy step-by-step construction. An example is schematic layouts or
architectural designs. Plans are created but nothing has been built yet.

The Director Chakra

Masculine

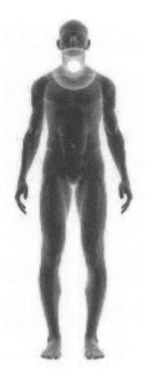

Location: The throat and thyroid

Function:

- Specifically communicates details with the voice.

- Detailed directions communicate the previous plans of the Power, Goal, and Decision Chakras.

In Balance: One will be able to clearly communicate plans and specifics by using schematics that list step-by-step orders to be completed.

The Connection Chakra

Feminine

Location: The heart, pericardium, and lungs

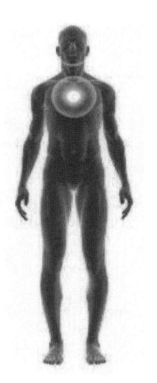

Function:

- The Connection Chakra is about communicating intentions and feelings often without saying a word or very few.

- It is soft and gentle which communicates the whole plan while empowering others.

In Balance: When this chakra is in balance one is intuitive and empathetic. One can express what is needed and can empower others by feeling what they can accomplish. They can express vulnerabilities with themselves and is able to ask for help from others when it is needed.

One would know the time to differentiate between empowering others to use their own skills or feeling obligated to do the things others can easily do themselves.

The Integrity Chakra

Feminine

Location: liver, gall bladder, and spleen

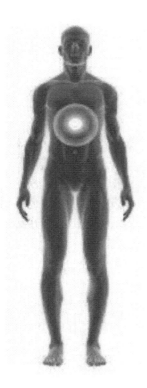

Function:

• The Integrity Chakra is the immune system of the body.

• In the manifestation process, this is where all plans are already completed and now it is time for the shovel to hit the ground.

• The Integrity Chakra makes the discernment if newly found choices are within the plan and purpose of the individual.

• If the new choices are within the plan and purpose, they will be implemented and anything less than the highest and best good will be discarded.

In Balance: When in balance one will have excellent discernment and knows their own limits. One will know the rules of energy and can moderate when to bend them and when to stand firm.

The Strength Chakra

Masculine

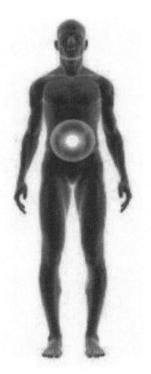

Location: pancreas, small intestines, stomach, and kidneys

Function:

- The power to move things into action.

- The ability to hold an intention to the end of completion without compromise.

- The beginning of manifesting ideas into the physical.

- The "Internal Battery" of the body.

In Balance: In perfect balance one will have true ability to manifest the plan into the physical plane with little effort. The individual will have the strength to hold the original plan from beginning to end.

The Passion Chakra

Masculine

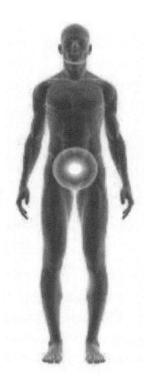

Location: large intestines

Function:

- Where things are expressed in an outward fashion into the world.
- Action is the name of the game and the plan will be completed.

In Balance: Ability to get up and go and accomplish the plans that one sets out to do.

The Love Chakra

Feminine

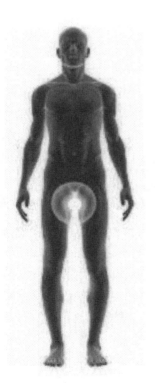

Location: The hips, bladder, and genitalia

Function:

- Showing and displaying how one feels through hugs, handshakes, physical affection, and sex.
- Letting things go, like when a mama bird pushes a baby bird out of the nest.

In Balance: One can genuinely express how one feels physically and are open to receive energy and love from others.

The Freedom Chakra

Masculine

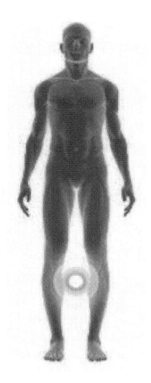

Location: Below the knees and upper calves

Function:

• The first chakra to receive the Female Energy Connection* from the Earth.

• Responsible for connecting to locations and committing to relationships.

• The last step of the manifestation process that lets go of everything, so it can go out and blossom into the world.

In Balance: One can accept any outcome and is also able to change one's situation in life with jobs,
relationships and ideas. One will be able to accept criticisms and react in a balanced thoughtful way. One will be able to have a healthy discernment of judgment with themselves and others.

(*See the Three Connections)

Characteristics of Male and Female Energy

Throughout this book will be references to the characteristics of Male and Female Energy. In the 10 Chakra Model, there are five pairs of male and female chakras. A pair will often be next to each other and they will complement each other just like the left and right hemispheres of the brain.

The Male Energy is the most praised and celebrated in the American culture as it is the one that is seen, and we can measure the results of it. Male Energy is loud, strong, bright, and full of action. The Female Energy has been suppressed as the human culture has been under a Patriarchal Rule. We are now entering a new consciousness where we will begin to swing back into Matriarchal Rule. Female Energy has not gotten the recognition of importance because it is a silent energy. It is about feeling, quiet, solitude, connection, and the "not doing" which is just "being."

In business, the Male Energy has dominated the landscape with bright lights, flash, and "how many quantities were made and how quickly was it done?" As most experience these successful results, one may notice after a while that there is something missing, the Female Energy. With this success of the Male Energy we must also connect with the Female Energy, and together, these energies lead to goals that are completed and are an accomplishment for all.

The new paradigm of business is to include the subtleties of the Female Energy, to connect with others on a higher level for deeper meaning and to understand why our business is important. Without the Female Energy, it is too easy to become greedy and cut-throat as one would not have to feel anything to keep this behavior up.

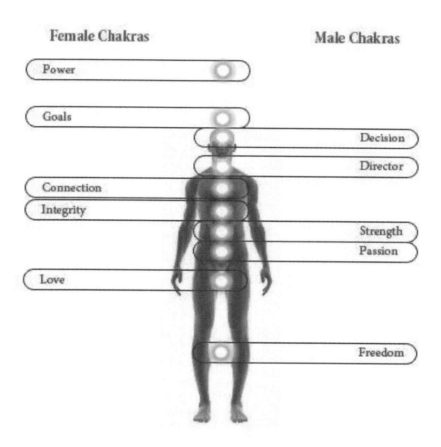

The balance of Male and Female Energy is imperative in living a meaningful and fulfilling life. As far as I am concerned, this is the most crucial element that one needs to recognize in this life. So many of us are running around lopsided in having either too much Male or Female Energy and wondering why nothing is working. By recognizing all the pieces and seeing how they go together, one can begin to take command of their life and change it for the better.

Male and Female Chakras work together in pairs

If one noticed in the list of chakras, each chakra was named masculine or feminine. One can put the pairs together to see how they work together and how one can benefit with the awareness of using both energies.

Goal and Decision Chakras

Strategy

These two chakras work with starting the initial intentions and envisioning the Plan. Visualizing, brainstorming and practiced scenarios are conjured up in these two chakras. The Feminine Goal Chakra starts with the feeling they want to have at the end of the original intention. The Masculine Decision Chakra comes up with different scenarios to manifest a plan of action that will support the Goal's feeling. In this illustration, the hiker is pointing the way by using the map to make the best decision to reach the end of the maze, which would be filled with joy.

Director and Connection Chakras

Communication

These two chakras are the communicators of the individuals plans to the outside world. The Director Chakra is masculine which will be very specific and detailed to what it wants to accomplish. Yes and No are clear in the Director Chakra and there is no room for maybe. The Connection Chakra is feminine which communicates by feeling. Through this silent communication, we can feel the intent of what one wants to communicate. Sometimes a smile or look from the eyes can communicate the intent of an individual. When they work together one will understand what the intent is of that person and the specifics of how to go about the task.

In the illustration, the man (Director Chakra) is initiating an action of love for the lady by presenting a rose (action). The lady (Connection Chakra) is already expressing the joy (feeling) for the relationship. Both are communicating their appreciation for each other.

Integrity and Strength Chakras

Rules

The plans have been thought of and communicated; now it is time for action. These chakras are about the practicality of physically creating the plan. Integrity, which is feminine, will be the one that will rate if the plans can stay within the rules, budget, and the thought of, "Can it be done?" The Strength Chakra, which is masculine, will use the appropriate force and action to move and adjust objects. The establishment of what can be done and what cannot be done will be defined by this pair of chakras.

In the illustration, Integrity and Strength are the immune system and act just like a brick wall. Integrity will be like the brick, already poised for strength and laying down the line. Strength is the mortar that grabs and adheres the bricks together creating a very long-lasting wall.

Passion and Love Chakras

Expression

The original intent of the feelings of the Goal and Connection Chakra will be expressed in the physical realm by the Passion and Love Chakra. Once plans have been created, the result will be expressed by these chakras. The Passion Chakra, which is masculine, is about outwardly expressing joy to others and

sharing the creation. The Love Chakra, which is feminine, expresses the love for the project and basks in the feeling of what was created.

In the illustration a couple is dancing. Typically, the Man leads, as does the Passion Chakra, a Male Energy, which directs and moves the couple all over the dance floor. The lady dancer, the Love Chakra, represents the Female Energy, by expressing how she feels. In dancing, it is usually the female's beauty and expression that is shown off as the male leads her around.

Power and Freedom Chakras

Time and Space

Power and Freedom both rule the edges of the top and bottom of the Aura. They help hold the place where the other chakras will be present in a specific and intentional time and space. Power, which is feminine, holds the Divine plan of the individual's intentions.

The Freedom Chakra, which is masculine, will look for the time and space for those intentions to manifest. The Freedom "to move" and the Power "to be" are necessary so that the other chakras will be able to express their full selves in the appropriate atmosphere.

In the previous illustration, a picture of our galaxy is showing that we have the Freedom to be anywhere we want. In our personal Power, we can choose where in time or space we would like to express our purpose.

The Three Connections

As above, so below - the melting of Unity

When we look at the 6-pointed stars, which is referred to as The Star of David or The Merkabah, it represents the chakra system and the human aura. The 6-pointed star has two triangles - one pointing up and one pointing down. The triangle pointing up represents the Female Energy. This represents Female Energy rising from the Earth. The triangle pointing down is the Male Energy. This is representing the Male Energy descending from the heavens towards Earth. All opposites in the universe that are equal in opposing energy will eventually merge and when they form together as One they will create a third object - like when the colors Yellow and Red are combined to create Orange. This is how our world is created; it is the merging of the Male and Female Energies. Everything that exists in our current plane is the result of Male and Female Energy equally combining and forming a new energy, entity, or dimension.

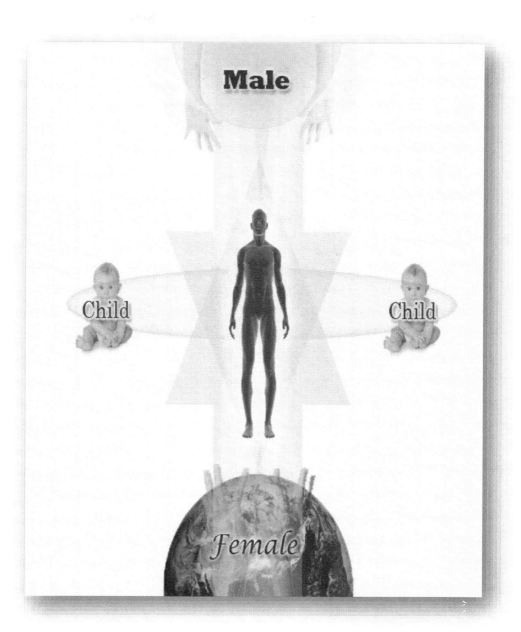

The Three Connections

Light Bulb anatomy and The Three Connections

To hold, light up, and support the 10 Chakra Model, it has to be connected to a higher source. Just like a light bulb there will be two wires, one positive and one negative that balance the energy to create light. This is the same thing that happens when the Male and Female Energy form together. The overlapping merging of this energy creates a third energy called the Child. The Child is the result of the merging energies of the Male and Female which creates this physical dimension that we all live in.

These Three Connections consist of the energies of Male, Female, and the Child. The Male Connection comes from above and enters the top pole of the aura. The Male Connection consists of your own soul's consciousness. In the Male Energy, all the information of the soul's purpose and objectives are in place for their time on Earth. The Female Connection which enters the bottom pole of the aura consists of the density rules of the planet one is on, and the rules of the body and how it is to be used. The Child Connection is the creation of the merging of the Male and Female and it creates space for them to coexist together. The Child Connection is where energies of the Male and Female mingle together and play on the big field of life, testing the parameters of their creations.

The Merkabah, the six-pointed star, has two triangles that spin horizontally together in perfect balance which creates a third plane. Once this balance is maintained, the Child Connection becomes of equal importance to the Connections of the Male and Female, and the establishment of the Three Connections is born.

The Three Connections is a support system for the 10 Chakra Model. The Three Connections are connecting the Universe to the 10 Chakra Model. Through the Three Connections, our energy is sourced and the way it is maintained. Through this pathway, we can connect with each other, the cosmos, and the Earth. By maintaining and affirming these connections we can achieve the feeling of being One with everything.

Other Examples of The Three Connections

Plants and trees also are in balance with the Three Connections. Leaves point upward and receive the Light which is Male Connection. The roots of plants dig into the Earth and receive the Female Connection. When these two energies have merged together in harmony they create a third energy, The Child Energy, which is the fruit and seeds which share and connect us all.

A laptop computer receives WIFI from the internet, a Male Connection. The power cord is the Female Connection. The computer screen, where we interface with one another and communicate information, is the Child Connection.

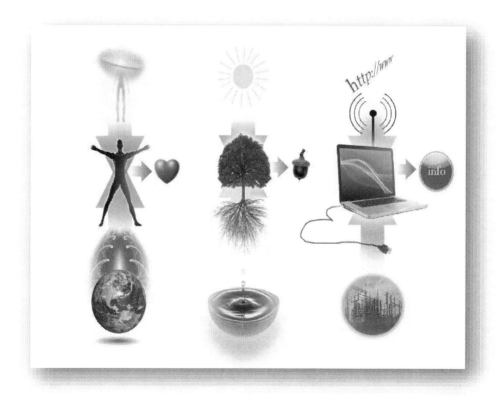

Thinkers and Doers

If we draw a line in the middle of the chakra system between the Connection Chakra and the Integrity Chakra, another characteristic emerges. We can break up the system into the Thinkers and the Doers. From the Connection Chakra and up, there is a lot of communicating and planning going on but essentially nothing has been implemented into action or manifested into the physical realm.

The chakras from the Power Chakra to the Connection Chakra are all about developing and planning what to create. Once that Plan has been developed it is then passed to the Doers. From the Integrity Chakra to the Freedom Chakra it is all about doing and bringing the Plan to life. The Doers do nothing about planning and developing, and they are essentially real-world testing to see if the Plan can be manifested.

> **Anxiety: [ang-zahy-i-tee] – noun, plural -ties. 1. When things don't go according to the Plan 2. When one decides to do everything by themselves.**

I have noticed a similarity among people with anxiety, when their Thinker-Doer Energy is not in balance. When manifesting an idea or plan, they will skip the Thinker/Planning stage and go right to the Doer Chakras. They think that if they look busy, that means they are actually doing something. However, once these systems have been repeated many times over, subconsciously they become worried because they know they are wasting their time. Sure, we have many options here on Earth, but if you are not living according to the Plan that you set out to do, subconsciously you know this and begin to worry.

When we can take a minute to slow down and focus on what our Plan is, then and only then should we start to act on it. Otherwise, we will waste a tremendous amount of time and resources "guessing" about what we should be doing. Then, after enough failures, the Doer will not want to make another decision because they know that they are going to waste even more time.

We need to align our Plan with our talents and failures. By aligning yourself with your Original Purpose, this will give ease to the Doers to be clear on what actions they need to make. When we are aligned with our Plan, we are aligned with the Source. At the Source is where everything comes from and when we acknowledge that we can't do it all by ourselves, then we can begin to live in peace rather than anxiety.

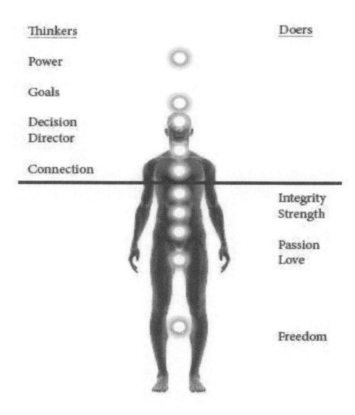

Knowing who you are and what you do

For one to fully create a Plan that succeeds, the balance of the Thinkers and Doers must be in harmony. If one is stronger or weaker than the other the Plan has the possibility of falling apart, never being done, or just runs into many difficulties.

One may be a better Doer than a Thinker and vice versa. So, it is best to collaborate with those that are stronger where one is weak. Creating a team where individuals are strong in different areas will create a balanced and successful project team.

The Numbers Have Meaning and Purpose

To manifest a plan or idea, when working with the 10 Chakra Model, it starts at the top with Purpose, the Power Chakra, and enters the physical realm through the Freedom Chakra. At first, I numbered the chakras from the 1-10 from the top down. However, after studying Numerology, I changed the numbers to start with 1 at the bottom (Freedom Chakra) and 10 at the top (Power Chakra). This change is inspired by Numerology as the definitions are the same as my 10 Chakra Model. This similarity I believe is another validation that there is some legitimate truth to the 10 Chakra model.

Glynis McCant, author of *Glynis has your Number*, is a numerologist, and in the next illustration I am referencing the Numerology definition from her book. There are parallels to Numerology, the 10 Chakra Model, and where numbers are found in nature. I believe all three models validate each other as no mere coincidence but to show us that everything in nature has the same order and purpose.

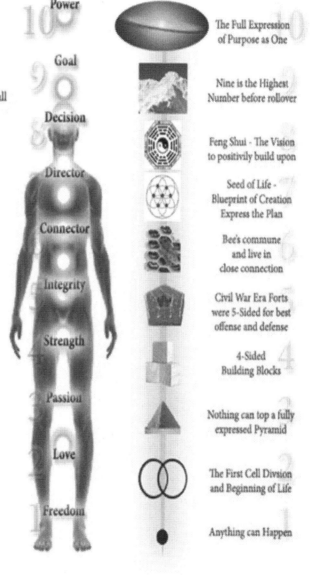

Chapter 2

Without One There is None

I believe one of the downfalls of the current Medical model is how we compartmentalize everything. There is a specialist for every disease and body part. Most physicians are so fixated on taking away the pain that they don't explore the root cause of it. I have learned to see things in their entirety and compartmentalizing never made sense to me. I was diagnosed "Learning Disabled" and Dyslexic while in grade school. The current and correct label, in my opinion, is Right-Brained. Today's school system is purely Left-Brained which is centered around lists and memorizing for the exercise of regurgitating what someone else says. Right–Brained thinking requires seeing how the entire system works together and seeks to understand the purpose of each part within the whole. It does take longer to understand the full picture but once the whole is understood it is easier to trouble shoot problems that come up. When we just memorize dates and lists, it is difficult to problem solve where an issue arises, which is often due to the system that precedes it. If there is a log blocking the stream upriver, downriver the river bed will dry up. In our current system, all emphasis is on fixing the dry river bed and making water appear in that area, when the real solution is simply moving a log that is upstream.

I believe this is the current trouble with today's guidance and health. So much focus is placed on the symptom and little effort is paid toward finding the cause. With every issue, there will always be two problems, the initial cause and the effect (symptom). Often, we just look at the effect and ignore the cause, but this technique will never solve the problem and the problem will continue to persist in diverse ways. In the Cause and Effect Section (Chapter 3) we will go over this subject in more detail. As for now, we are going to focus on the importance of the whole.

The Universe and the human body are very adaptable and can dip and shimmy their way through demanding situations. There are multiple solutions to every problem and if we can understand the Divine Plan we will notice that when one area fails another area will make up for it. This adaption to circumstance is very important, however, when an area is repeatedly beaten down without the shimmy, areas can wear out and die. Often, we just want to ignore these areas as they appear to have no solution, or it just seems there is no possible easy solution. I believe we are here for a greater purpose which is to understand how the Universe works. The Human Experiment is a playground for us to personally understand our own lessons and observe how the Universe works. So, when a problem is put it front of us, if we acknowledge we put it there for our spiritual evolution, then we can understand how to persevere through a situation and not go into victimhood.

I believe one of the main goals of the Human Experiment is to balance our Spirit with our Human physical form. Just like the Male and Female Triangles that form the Merkabah that (discussed in Chapter 1). When these two entities perfectly balance themselves together we will achieve a greater sense of purpose. To understand how we do this to ourselves, we need to understand that we create the universe around us and circumstances that are created around us. When we can see that we create our problems, then we can see what the solutions are. When we can look at our pain as guidance, we can see how we may not be playing the human game correctly and that we just drew the "lost a turn" card. The Universe is always instructing us on which way to go and if we can look at drawbacks as assets we can more clearly see the path ahead of us.

So, if we can recognize the repeated failures and see where we consistently get things wrong, then we can strengthen our weaknesses shift our paradigm and start to see them as strengths. Knowing when to ask for help where you are weak makes you stronger.

In the chakra system, each chakra has a specific task to do within a desired manifestation. For a temporary amount of time a chakra can do the task of another chakra. If a chakra goes out of commission due to overuse or suppression, another chakra will make up for it by doing something else. However, the human experiment for evolution requires all your chakras to be fully expressed, and this is how one will master this human experience and move up through their evolutionary experience. So, it is okay to temporarily use a part of yourself to support another part; however, there is a limit to this adaption. If it becomes expected to comprise your energies, they will eventually wear out and not work properly. This is akin to a baker filling in for a plumber. Sure, the baker can cut a pipe or two but eventually he will wear out in more extreme conditions. This is often what happens to a Too Strong Chakra that must fill in for a Too Weak suppressed chakra. The once Strong Chakra will become weak and tired and then another chakra that is not suited for the job will also become tired.

With every manifestation, there is a beginning and an ending. If the original intention never gets fulfilled, that means somewhere in the process something failed. In the 10 Chakra model, it is imperative that all the chakras do their part so that the sum of all their energy is expressed fully. If one goes down, then they all go down, and frustration and anxiety will be the only result.

In the chakra scene, there are a couple of popular chakras that get most of the attention like the Heart (Connection Chakra) and the Third Eye (Decision Chakra). A lot of focus will be placed on these two, however, when we put one chakra ahead of another we lose the bigger picture and we will continually fail in completing the original intention. I believe this is so because we do not understand what they do. The Third Eye chakra is popular because it is directly involved with our intuition (and one can put an eyeball sticker between their eyes which is fun for parties and Halloween). The Heart is popular because most think it is the most important of all chakras and drawing the heart symbol is quite powerful. However, the supporting chakras help communicate and strengthen the Heart and Third Eye's intention. Without them, the popular chakras will never be heard or seen. Each chakra is important, and all must be fully expressed without putting one above another, otherwise the original intention will be imbalanced, and the manifestation will not be expressed.

The Manifestation of Wooing a Lady

The first illustration is about a man wanting to woo his lady by surprising her with a picnic. The original intention of the man is to impress his lady, so they can have a bonding and romantic experience. The illustration will show how each chakra represents a piece of creating the picnic event, from the original intention to the result of the manifestation.

Note: The illustration has been arranged in a 2-Dimensional view; in that each action in the picture is in line horizontally with the corresponding chakra.

We start at the top with the Power Chakra (chakra number 10). Your Power represents the things that no one can take from you like your name, talents, values, and all your beliefs. In this case, this man is a sailor and cook, and he wants to express this in a romantic way, so he chooses this scenario to impress his lady by providing an adventure on the ocean to a remote island where a nice picnic awaits.

Next is the Goal Chakra (9). The man wants to come up with a plan that makes his lady feel like the goddess that she is and so this trip will be very impressive to her. He has already examined what has impressed her and this trip will make her feel very appreciative, special, and she will feel that everything is safe...which is the Goal.

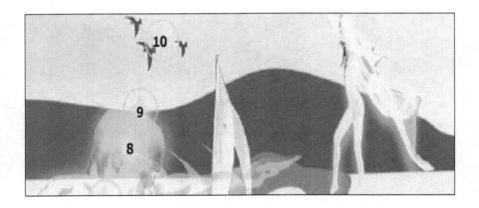

The Decision Chakra (8) is involved in planning and envisioning the logistics of how to collaborate this adventure. The thought process may be: She is over there - How do I pick her up and what is the best mode of transportation? How am I going to pick her up, and what time? What flowers am I bringing her? The food should be set and ready. I must pick her up at this time, so we can get to the island by sunset. Not much emotion is in this chakra and it is all about planning the actions and prioritizing them.

The Director Chakra (7) will express the specifics of the plan to the other person involved. In the scenario, the man is going to tell the lady, "I am going to pick you up in a boat at 9:00am and we are going to sail around for a while and then I have a surprise for you." In the illustration, the wind is representing movement and for the first time the plan is given away to another.

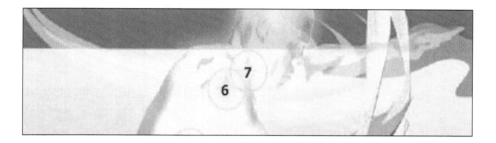

The Connection Chakra (6) is related to connecting to others. The Director Chakra is expressing its specific plans and the Connection Chakra is feeling the other party's reaction to the plans by asking questions such as, do they understand what I am saying? Do they like what I am saying? Are we in agreement? Once the two parties agree and fully understand the plans, both can feel content and empowered about their future.

The Connection Chakra or Heart is represented in the illustration by the wind hitting the sails of the boat. Is the impact of the wind gentle enough on the sails to ensure the boat makes it safely to the other side? Connecting and trusting one another is communicating without speaking, which is what the Heart is about.

When we cross in the realm of the lower chakras, the first one is the Integrity Chakra (5), the planning is done and now it is time for action. That action is dependent on following the rules of the original intention. When it comes to integrity it is all about committing to the agreed upon plans, so that trust is established with the other party.

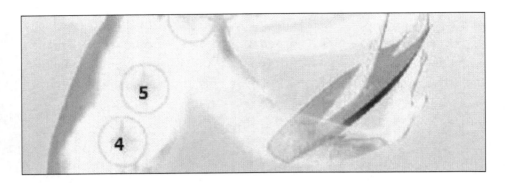

The Integrity and Strength Chakra (4) represents the quality of the boat. Integrity can represent that the right kind of boat is used for the desired job. A couple of questions that be asked are, "Will this boat hold two people safely and will this impress the lady and make her feel safe as the Goal Chakra first intended?"

The Strength Chakra represents the ability to hold things together. "Is this boat strong enough to sustain the journey?" For the man, we might wonder, does he have the strength to follow through with the plans and make everything happen that he promised to do? Strength is the endurance of sticking with the plan all the way to the end. The balance of the initial plan must be in balance with the reality of "can I make this happen?" At this point we will see if one can do what they say, or are they all talk?

The Passion Chakra (3) may be measured in the extravagant details of the date. Passion is about being in an expressive outgoing movement. For example, Passion for the picnic may be what the man did to set it up. Did he get just enough food, a ratty blanket, and a small fire? Or did he go to the extreme and bring many candles, a violin orchestra, and a firework display. These are all outward examples of passion being expressed and are all dependent on the original intention.

The Love Chakra (2) is the expression of physical feelings on the physical level. Tasting the food at the picnic, being in companionship with the one you are with, and feeling the warmth of the fire are all part of this expression. The balance of the Passion and Love Chakras are measured here. How much did the man really need to do or bring to reach the desired impression from his lady? Does the initial energy of the plan balance the amount of energy that was put into it?

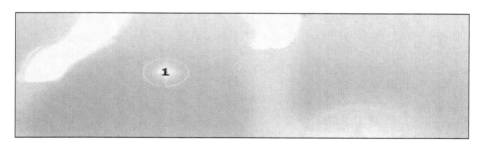

Lastly, is to consider the Freedom Chakra (1). From the outside edges of the Aura to the middle, a similar theme happens. The outside edge chakras, the Power and Freedom Chakra, together, create the supporting edges of the intention and as we move to the center of the Aura, the chakras become very specific.

The Freedom Chakra is concerned with the ability to move in any direction. In this scenario, the man can choose any direction or event to express what he would like to do with his lady. In this scenario, he chooses a picnic with a sailboat ride. The Freedom of sailing the boat to whichever path the man chooses to go in is the Freedom Chakra. The Power Chakra holds the space of what the man can do with his talents and the Freedom Chakra holds the physical plane on which the original intention is expressed.

The Three Connections

How the 10 Chakras attach to the Universe

Along with the 10 Chakras are The Three Connections. The Three Connections hold the Intention together in Space.

At the very top of the illustration we have two hands coming down from the sky. This represents the Male Connection which is the Source of all knowledge and energy. The Male energy is often referred to as light and in this illustration, it is the sun shining on the whole scene.

In the middle, often referred to as the solar plexus, is the Child Connection. This is the Earthly plane where we all meet and converse with each other. In the illustration, we have a dog and a whale representing our friends and fellow Earth mates.

This connection helps the scenario by making suggestions for the date and it is like consulting a friend for advice. For example, "You could take her on a sailboat ride, make a picnic, and make sure she is not allergic to that cheese you just bought." We reference the Child Connection for help on the Earthly plane to help us choose the right tools for our intentions.

Finally, we get to the Feminine Connection. Often, she is considered last, although at the same time she is first...as all things begin and end here. The Feminine Connection is the manifestation of physical solid objects. In this illustration, she represents the earth and all materials used in the previous scenario.

As we can see, each area displayed has a very distinct role in supporting the scenario in the illustration. Without any one of the Connections or Chakras, the date would not happen. One chakra is not any more important than the other. If we look at taking one area away we can see how the whole scenario will fall apart.

Without the Power Chakra – The man would have no clue as to what to do.

Without the Goal Chakra – The man would have not known why he should complete anything and that he wanted a mate.

Without the Decision Chakra – The man would not have been able to decide how the plan should take place and how it should be best carried out.

Without the Direction Chakra – Without the time and specific date how would the couple meet?

Without the Connection Chakra – The man needs to know what the woman wants otherwise how do they know they should be together.

Without the Integrity Chakra – There would be no boat or vessel to impress the woman and get her to the picnic.

Without the Strength Chakra – The man would not have been able to stay on track with the plan, so all material can be used as it was intended.

Without the Passion Chakra – There would be no picnic and the man would not be able to celebrate the woman.

Without the Love Chakra – The man would not be able to feel how the woman feels toward him.

Without the Male Connection – There would be no light or knowledge to guide the man and let him know what to do or where to go.

Without the Child Connection – The man would not have asked others for help and guidance in carrying out his plan for the woman.

Without the Female Connection – The man would have no planet to stand on and he would be floating in space without a physical body.

Chapter 3

The Too Strong & Too Weak Chakras

Cause, Effects, and Balance

In every issue with a disease, pain, or argument there always seems to be two sides; winning vs. losing, conquered vs. defeated, right vs. wrong, push vs. pull, loud vs. quiet, strong vs. weak, and greedy vs. poor. An increase in drama and excitement equate to chakras that are out of balance.

In this dualistic universe, there are always two sides to every issue and the discussion continues that one side is always better than the other and that it is very important to always be on the winning side. It is very important to envision the bigger picture for humanity, that there is never really a winner or loser and that balance is key. When it comes to health, if we have one part of our body losing and the other winning, it will eventually add up to our health losing. This can also be demonstrated in relationships, especially when we decide that it is always the other person's fault. With enough reflection, we can see that in nearly every conflict both parties are equally responsible.

In my massage practice, I have observed that my clients usually cause the pain themselves by not paying attention to how their bodies work and they ignore the importance of self-care and rest.

In the mechanics of the body, for every muscle group that pulls an appendage in a certain direction, there will be another group of muscles on the other side of the body that will pull the appendage in the opposite direction.

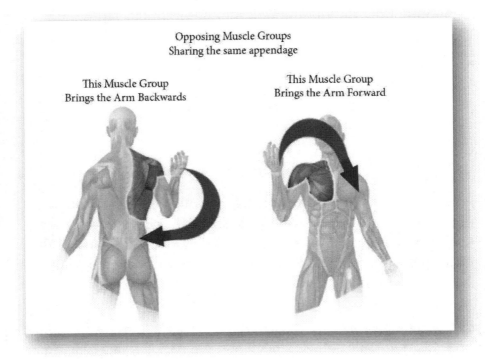

There is a tissue layer called fascia that is in-between the skin and the muscles. It is a thin web-like membrane that connects the muscles together to the inner layer of the skin. If one muscle group becomes compromised it will affect the opposing group.

In the illustration, the shortened overused chest muscle will pull the shoulders forward. The strain of this action will affect the shoulders in the back area by overstretching them. Whenever a muscle is over-stretched the muscle is being pulled away from the bone and the stress causes the pain that we feel. The problem in this case is that the overused chest muscle does not relay any pain. We often rub the back of our shoulder where the pain is but unfortunately relief will not come anytime soon. The real culprits in the matter are the chest muscles. To relieve the painful back muscles, we need to first stretch out the chest muscles, then flex and shorten the back muscles thus putting them back into their original position, which will help to alleviate the pain.

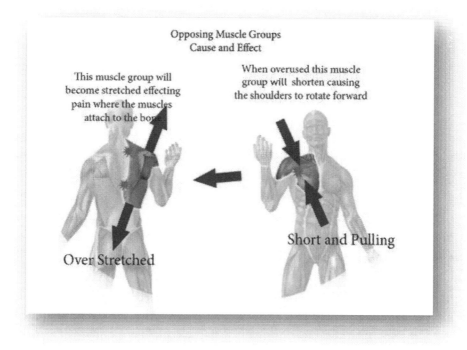

Solutions – Awareness and Technique

To help solve the tug-a-war of a muscle group we need to look at the big picture. We need to acknowledge the concept that when there is a pain or disease, it is usually caused by something else. Proper body mechanics and self-awareness are two workable solutions to help prevent a lot of these imbalances.

If you are in physical pain, you may be aware that the techniques you are using in your daily life need improving. Perhaps you are sitting at your desk with incorrect posture for too long without a break, or you realize that you need a lesson on the correct technique when beginning a new exercise. This is the time to stop and change your alignment to a safer one; with self-awareness of the use of your body, you can change your future and not hurt yourself any further. When we wait for things to break, we have ignored the warning signs and now we must take a mandatory health time-out.

The Energetics of Cause and Effect

In my Medical Intuitive sessions with my clients I can observe the invisible energetic realm and help people see the cause and effect they are creating in their lives. I have found that no issue, disease, or injury is random and just shows up because you innocently walk down the street, or it is strictly genetic. With every choice, thought, and action you make, you are creating health or dis-ease in your body. Sometimes people like to blame genetics for their health problems, such as repeatedly saying, "This disease is in my family line, so I also have it." Science has countered this reasoning with Epigenetics, with its main premise being that we can change our genes with our minds. We may have inherited certain genetic predispositions to diseases, however, we can change our genes by changing inherited behavior. Genetics can be controlled by thought, emotions, sound vibrations, and the very words we repeat to ourselves every day.

For every issue I have worked on with a client, there is always a message behind the pain. I can intuitively see what the energy is around an issue and sometimes I can hear and feel the voices from angry people and the inner voice of the individual reacting to other people or from their own personal guilt.

When we shut down a part of ourselves, we do this either to protect ourselves from not wanting to see something or we are afraid of making someone mad. When we shut down an energy system, then another system must kick in double time to make up for it. The cause of how we compromise ourselves will affect our health and daily lives.

Two Chakras for Every Issue – The Too Strong & Too Weak

In my sessions with clients we address the issues that they wish to work through and heal. For every issue I work on, there will always be two chakras that are affected; the one that has been turned off or suppressed (Too Weak), and the one that must make up for it (Too Strong). A chakra that is turned off is Too Weak and the chakra that makes up for that one is Too Strong. When a chakra reaches the "Too" status it is not good even if it is Too Strong. When energy is Too Strong it is like concrete that has been mixed together with too much hardener, which will make the concrete brittle and crack easier. Also, a Too Strong Chakra will become exhausted very quickly and it will run out of steam. For one chakra to do the work of two is very exhausting and it is like one hand lifting the load that is meant for two hands.

The main point is to recognize that in every imbalance there is a Too Weak Chakra coupled with a Too Strong Chakra. Just like the previous examples of the opposing muscle groups, when one side pushes too hard the other side will stretch and break.

Our chakras should ebb and flow as we move through life. As we learn and forgive others, our chakras move like trees in the wind bending with the times. However, when we experience a trauma such as being assaulted, being yelled at or we hurt ourselves, then fear can set in and the chakra energy will freeze. The unwillingness to process this event will lead a chakra to become stuck or frozen at the time when the trauma or injury took place. We then move through life forgetting or not wanting to remember the event and we suppress it. Our chakras that are stuck in fear will later manifest themselves through diseases or repetitive mistakes. The universe is always trying to help us by reminding us we have unfinished business and it gives us the opportunity to resolve our fears and traumas. We need all our chakras turned on and spinning in balance for us to realize our full spiritual potential. To evolve our conscious minds, we need to have a high vibrational frequency, so we can continually progress. When we are stuck in fear and anger we will have a low frequency. It is my personal belief that the most important thing to do in this lifetime is to balance our chakras where they all spin at the same rate. This conscious evolutionary process involves forgiving ourselves and others. Don't be concerned with how others progress or try to teach anyone else a lesson – focus on self-evolution. Everyone grows at their own pace. I believe in the law of karma and if you do not learn your lessons now, you will get the opportunity later in this lifetime or a future lifetime.

We are here to learn how life evolves and functions. Everyone has signed up for this Human experiment and no one gets to leave until they are balanced.

The Too Strong and Too Weak

The Too Strong and Too Weak labels are to help identify the condition of a chakra. As I mentioned before, every issue a person is dealing with has a Too Strong Chakra and a Too Weak Chakra. These labels would not be necessary if we could learn from our lessons and identify our surroundings and be able to change with life. However, many of our issues are due to a trauma at an early age or from the manipulated guidance that society, parents, or religion gives us. People are highly skeptical of what to believe. So now it comes down to the new common religion, Spirituality, which means one has no religion but accepts all faiths and belief systems without judgment. A spiritual person is self-aware of their presence in life and accepts responsibility for what they create and manifest.

As we move through life, our traumas go with us and the stuck chakras remain Strong and Weak until we can identify them and let go of our past. It is tough to identify these issues ourselves because there aren't enough balanced people around to be good examples. We learn behaviors from our imbalanced parents, teachers, and politicians, or anyone else that influences us. It is the crazy following the crazy. We need to stop this merry-go-round and recognize that as we change ourselves, that will inspire others to change as well. A truly self-responsible person is a powerful creator of their life and destiny. One of the greatest gifts one can give to the world is to be the example of one who is balanced in all aspects of life; this is how one can truly help humanity.

Attracting the Too Strong and the Too Weak

The chakra that is Too Strong always gets the attention because it is the one that is angry and loud. Often the Too Strong Chakra is the symptom of the issue. Regularly the Too Weak Chakra is the cause, but because it is turned off we do not get to hear the voice of it and it is ignored.

Often it will be recognized in what we attract to us. Where we are Too Strong in a chakra, we will attract someone who is equally Too Weak in the same chakra. Our weakness will be shown to us by the Universe through the situations we attract. It will manifest as an angry boss or a relationship with someone who keeps yelling and nagging at us, ultimately showing us our weaknesses. If they are yelling at you, perhaps it is because you are incapable of communicating what you're really feeling regarding a critical issue. Often the yelling and loud part gets all the blame, however the silent, nonresponsive and passive part is equally to blame.

Your Weakness is your Strength

A chakra is considered Too Strong when it generates more energy than the average of all chakra energy combined. When all the chakras are resonating at an equal resonance, this is balance. When one chakra resonates stronger than the overall balance, another chakra will have less energy as the "extra" goes to the one that is commanded to be brighter thus it gets stronger.

We ebb and flow and use distinct parts of ourselves during the day, however, when these chakras become stuck in Too Strong/Weak positions, this is when we will start to attract less than favorable conditions.

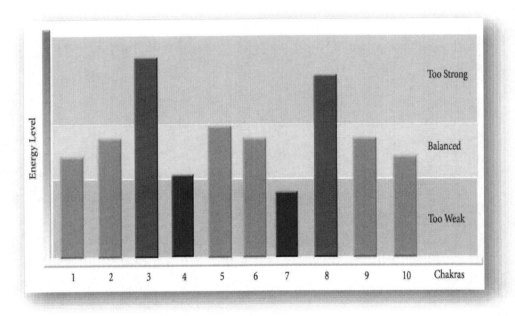

When too much energy is generating out of a single chakra it is considered Too Strong. The body and mind are working hard in this Too Strong area and desperately channeling too much energy into one chakra. Our strengths and talents are naturally amplified through Too Strong Chakras. In challenging situations, we will depend on our talents and strengths, however, these times are meant for our weaknesses to develop and persevere. When we are turn other chakras off and only depend on our strengths, we will soon lose the passion that we once had for the things we love. All our chakras need to burn brightly and evenly, and when one must shine to make up for others, that chakra will slowly die out quicker than the rest.

We are only as strong as the weakest link

It is very important to find and strengthen our weakness and not only depend on our strengths. We need to look at the times when we are challenged, which reminds us that we need to develop the weakest part of ourselves and not go into victimhood, whereby we perpetuate the drama filled merry-go-round.

We should celebrate and explore our talents but always remain mindful that we are living in a state of balance which creates perfect health. When our energy is Too Weak, we do not have enough energy generating out of a single chakra. This may result in the chakra not being expressed at all. We may turn a chakra off to give energy to a chakra that is Too Strong. This type of situation will manifest into potential problems if they continue to be out of balance for an extended period.

Chakras that are Too Weak can be inherited through learned behavior, personal soul lessons for growth, or appeasing someone else. A common issue I see in my practice is people turning off a chakra to appease someone else. This is common amongst children as they are so desperate to fit in with those around them. Children will do almost anything to better the world and if turning off a part of themselves will help, they will do it.

One may say to a part of themselves that is Too Weak, "Oh, I am just not good at that, so I will not try." This is a very disempowering statement, regardless of whether it's true. In my personal experience, every time I have worked on a part of myself that was weak I would always have huge benefits for persevering through the issue. As a holistic healer, it is imperative to work on your own weakness, otherwise how can you truly help another strive towards

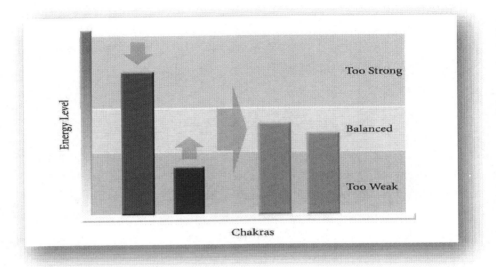

healing if you avoid it yourself? I have achieved so much success and knowledge by working through my issues that now I look forward to the next one. I was surprised recently when a friend of mine pushed my button. I thought I had none left to be pushed. It took me almost a month to figure out my issue but once I did it was easier to forgive that person and myself.

When we can recognize our weakness, this will give rest to our talents that are Too Strong. This will result in less chance of burn out and at the end of the day joy and rest will be easier to attain. Continually strengthening your strengths makes you weaker. Strengthening your weakness makes you stronger. Forgiving others and yourself makes you stronger. Asking for help makes you stronger.

Note for upcoming set of pictures:

Each of the Too Strong and Too Weak examples are extremes for each chakra. One does not have to always be identified with these characteristics all the time and every minute. Sometimes we may be peaceful 95% of the time but it is the remaining 5% that really tells us what we need to work on. It takes careful examination and honestly to recognize and step out of potential drama filled situations.

I have created a Facebook App that corresponds with this chapter. The App asks 20 questions that correspond with each of the 10 chakras. You may want to look at the attached worksheet at the end of the chapter or go through the app first so you won't be biased when answering the questions. If one looks for my Facebook Fanpage "The Aura of Attraction" - Jacob Caldwell" or on www.JacobCaldwell.com you will find the App there.

It is suggested that before you take the Aura of Attraction Survey, follow instructions 1-2 first. Take the Survey and then follow Instructions 3-6.

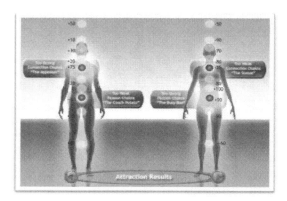

Aura of Attraction Survey   www.JacobCaldwell.com

1. I am in control of my life and I am in-line with my purpose.
2. I feel powerless in life and cannot do anything to improve the situations I am in.
3. I can make myself happy and usually have favorable outcomes.
4. I rely on others and circumstances to make me happy.
5. I know how I want to be and choose how I live my life.
6. I let others choose for me - like dinner, plans and events.
7. I am able to specifically articulate what I want.
8. I generally assume others know what is best for me.
9. I choose the terms on how I want to help others.
10. I feel obligated to help everyone in need even though it wears on me.
11. I am able to say, "No", and enforce my personal boundaries.
12. I often say, "That's OK", when others do what they want, even if it means I feel walked on.
13. I prefer to take a stand in the moment for what I feel is right and do not waiver.
14. I allow stronger people to go first and have their way.
15. I take the initiative and express what I like and don't like.
16. I feel too tired to move and I will do it later.
17. I am comfortable initiating physical contract, like hugs and handshakes.
18. I am uncomfortable with physical affection towards others and do not want to impose.
19. I am open to trying things differently and I am open to unexpected outcomes - good or bad.
20. I often feel trapped, like I will never get out of a situation and will have to put up with it.

60

Aura of Attraction Survey   www.JacobCaldwell.com

1. I am in control of my life and I am in-line with my purpose.
2. I feel powerless in life and cannot do anything to improve the situations I am in.
3. I can make myself happy and usually have favorable outcomes.
4. I rely on others and circumstances to make me happy.
5. I know how I want to be and choose how I live my life.
6. I let others choose for me - like dinner, plans and events.
7. I am able to specifically articulate what I want.
8. I generally assume others know what is best for me.
9. I choose the terms on how I want to help others.
10. I feel obligated to help everyone in need even though it wears on me.
11. I am able to say, "No", and enforce my personal boundaries.
12. I often say, "That's OK", when others do what they want, even if it means I feel walked-on.
13. I prefer to take a stand in the moment for what I feel is right and do not waiver.
14. I allow stronger people to go first and have their way.
15. I take the initiative and express what I like and don't like.
16. I feel too tired to move and I will do it later.
17. I am comfortable initiating physical contact, like hugs and handshakes.
18. I am uncomfortable with physical affection towards others and do not want to impose.
19. I am open to trying things differently and I am open to unexpected outcomes - good or bad.
20. I often feel trapped, like I will never get out of a situation and will have to put up with it.

Instructions for the Aura of Attraction Survey

1. In the "Aura of Attraction Survey" it is very important to be honest with your true self.

2. Read each of the 20 statements and circle the 0-100 scale with how much you agree with the statement.

   0 for Never, 50 Sometimes, 100 All the time.

Note: Think of yourself on an average in life of how well you relate to each statement. Try to avoid scoring all 100 and 0 unless you are truly Buddha or Jesus.

3. After you have taken the Survey you may notice that every two statements are in a group. To the far right is a green box.

   Add up the totals for each pair of statements.

The top statement is a positive statement and the lower statement is negative. If the top statement is larger than the sum total it will be positive (+).

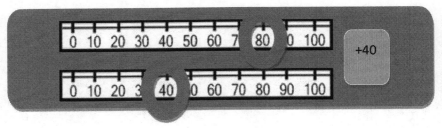

If the lower statement score is larger than the higher number, then the score will be negative (-).

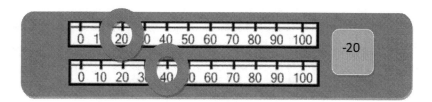

4. Observe all the scores in the far-right box. Circle the Largest (+) score and the Lowest (-) score.

5. **The Highest score will be your Too Strong Chakra and the Lowest Score will be your Too Weak Chakra. Re-read the Chapter to find your personal chakra pattern.**

6. Use the numbers to the left below ox to correspond to the chakra list of the Too Strong and Too Weak.

Later in the book we will go over how we attract energy to us. Your Highest Score will attract someone who has that same score as their Lowest Score. And if their Highest Score is in line with your Lowest Score then you two will be a "Perfect Match".

From the "Aura of Attraction" App, more in-depth information about the survey.

Ahead are a list of examples of all the chakras and the characteristics that someone with a Too Strong and Too Weak Chakra possess. These are meant to inspire one to recognize where their everyday issues may lie. An exercise to help one identity their own issues is to imagine a time where someone or something really bothered you and look for that characteristic in the Too Strong section. Then go through the Too Weak section and see where you reacted with one of those characteristics.

Becoming self-aware of what we do and taking responsibility for when we are Too Strong or Too Weak is a breakthrough on your journey to personal empowerment. Releasing judgment and enacting forgiveness and love without a reason will release one from their karmic wheel and one can begin a joyous, genuine, and purposeful life.

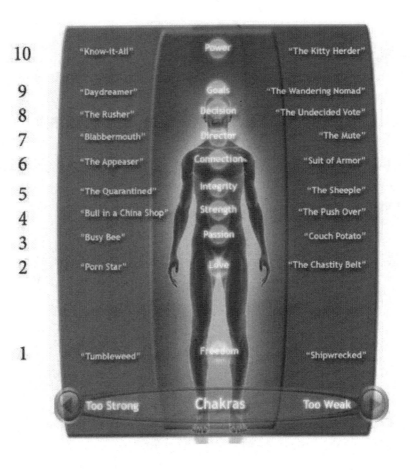

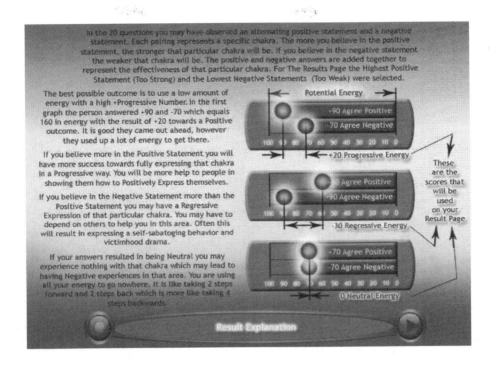

Notes of Graphical Illustration

Numbers will represent the specific chakra.

A Circle around that number will represent a Too Strong Chakra.

A Square around that number will represent a Too Weak Chakra.

The Circle and Square will be used in all the other illustrations throughout the book as well.

THE TOO STRONG

That's good, right?

Too Strong Power Chakra: "The Know-it-All"

A Too Strong Power Chakra requires having a very large and self-serving ego that "Knows-it-All". The "Know-it-All" needs to establish and prove to everyone how smart they are, because somewhere in life they may have had some trauma where a lot of their power was taken away. They will risk making a fool of themselves to appear smarter if enough people believe them to be the expert. These types have a tough time asking for help and would rather do it all themselves, because asking for help may reveal they don't know it all, and their identity would disappear.

In the illustration, the man has run out of gas and he is pushing his car through traffic, refusing the help of anyone as he thinks he can do it better by himself.

Physical Manifestation: Egotist

Too Strong Goal Chakra: "The Daydreamer"

When the Goal Chakra is Too Strong it can lead one into extreme day dreaming. These types of people will dream all day without caring if they accomplish anything. They are so impressed with their own dreams and thoughts that they sometimes think they do not have to do anything else. They are idealists that lack the motivation and practicality to make things happen in the real world.

Physical Manifestation: Head in the clouds and don't accomplish mush on the physical.

Too Strong Decision Chakra: "Rush Hour"

People who are Too Strong in the Decision Chakra tend to be very mental and live too much in their heads. These types think they have it all figured out and tend to assume others know what they are thinking and feeling. They will often get upset when people do not understand their needs, as they assume people should be able to read their minds. They will tend to be in a rush but will often be too early and miss out on the opportunity that has not quite manifested.

In the illustration, the "Rush Hour" man is so caught up in trying to get to work that sometimes vital details are overlooked...like pants!

Physical Manifestation: Often are the Cause of Car Accidents

Too Strong Director Chakra: "Blabber Mouth"

The "Blabber Mouth" is someone who talks on and on but may not know the point of their story, so they will talk until someone stops them or they reach some sort of conclusion. Sometimes the point is never reached as they often do not know what they are talking about. The "Blabber Mouth" wants to avoid silence and the feeling of insecurity this may bring, so they will engage in any conversation on any topic to distract themselves from feeling lonely or un-important. Often the "Blabber Mouth" doesn't know how to accomplish anything, as they are so caught up in the mental aspect of their lives that they never come down to earth long enough to complete a project or manifest one of their many dreams or ideas.

Physical Manifestation:
Hypothyroidism

Too Strong Connection Chakra: "The Appeaser"

"The Appeaser" is one of the most common imbalances, especially amongst women. These types trick themselves into thinking that doing everything for everyone is how they can best be of service to humanity. They have an innate ability to want to help others, but do not understand that by overextending themselves and by helping every stray dog on the street, they will soon have nothing but a thousand dogs in their back yard. It is important to take care of oneself and to be healthy and balanced before helping others. People who are constantly giving more than they are receiving will eventually burn out and have absolutely nothing left for themselves. In this imbalance, it is important for the person to begin teaching and empowering others to care themselves, as this is the true purpose of the Connection Chakra. The very popular saying, "Teach people how to fish so they can fish for themselves," is a powerful lesson for "The Appeaser."

In the illustration "The Appeaser" will give everything away until their wallet is empty, and their energy is spent.

Physical Manifestation:

   Breast Cancer

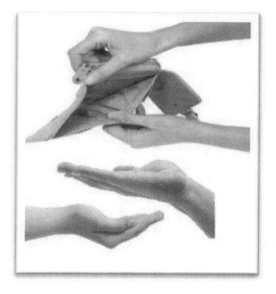

Too Strong Integrity Chakra: "Quarantined"

The Integrity Chakra is like a castle wall. When the self-created castle wall becomes Too Strong and impenetrable, the person will tend to shut off communication with the outside world. If one makes the walls around themselves Too Strong, one will soon become isolated, overprotected, and self-quarantined. Paranoia and fear is a common characteristic, as the person will only assume what others are thinking and feeling based upon their own fears and not on true reality.

Physical Manifestation: Liver Disease

Too Strong Strength Chakra: "Bull in a China Shop"

A Too Strong Strength Chakra comes from dominate behavior where empathy is lacking, and goals are achieved through forceful action. This imbalance is very common with men who are afraid to appear weak or have not learned to embrace their feminine side. There is no subtlety or gentleness with the "Bull in the China Shop", as something almost always gets broken. This is a very common attribute of the mentality of War, which is based on fear and greed with no regard for justice and balance. These types of people feel the need to do everything themselves. They often force plans or events together which usually ends up in something being broken, and frequent misunderstandings and power struggles occur as a result. Empathy is lacking in this person, as they just want the job done as quickly as possible with few regards as to who gets trampled along the way.

Physical Manifestation: Stomach Ulcers & Kidney Stones

Too Strong Passion Chakra: "Busy Bee"

People with a Too Strong Passion Chakra keep themselves very busy by running around and doing a million different things at once. They are always doing, doing, doing! These people are so addicted to keeping busy that they have lost track of what their real purpose is. All of the projects and running around are just distractions keeping them from their life's purpose. The "Busy Bee" may be good at many things, however, if their projects are not in line with their soul's purpose then they are simply wasting their time. These people need to slow down, take a deep breath, and ask themselves if everything they are doing is really in alignment with their goals and true reason for being alive.

Manifestation: Digestion Issues – Crohn's Disease & Ulcerative Colitis

Too Strong Love Chakra: "Porn Star"

The "Porn Star" is only concerned with having material objects, feeling good and having lots of sex. These types equate sex for love which is actually a distraction from their true suppressed feelings about themselves. The "Porn Star" may have learned these skills because they were taught only physical things can make one happy. Having money, an expensive car, and a big house also shows other people that they are important as well as proving it to themselves. These people are always seeking approval from others through sex, status and the accumulation of material objects. They want to feel good in the moment and are not concerned with their own conscious evolution.

Manifestation: Sexually Transmitted Diseases

Too Strong Freedom Chakra: "Tumbleweed"

A person with a Too Strong Freedom Chakra can be like a Tumbleweed drifting from place to place and person to person. If one is Too Strong in Freedom, this can lead to being non-committal, not finishing anything, or being so aloof that they miss out on real connections with people. Personal freedom can be very healthy if the person is truly following their heart and life's purpose. Excess freedom can lead to loneliness and isolation if the person never settles down, learns to grow and matures with a partner, or co-creates in a business.

Manifestation: Aloof, Depression

THE TOO WEAK

"Is that bad?"

Too Weak Power Chakra: "The Kitty Herder"

"The Kitty Herder" needs to control everything outside themselves because they cannot control anything inside of them self. Trying to control all things around oneself is nearly impossible. The need to control what your friends think and feel, is just too much work for any one person to do.

Since the "Kitty Herder" has little power to protect themselves, they feel they need to be proactive by influencing people on how to behave. With millions of people and opinions in the world, trying to control all things around oneself becomes impossible, just like herding cats.

Manifestation: Insecurity, Anxiety

Too Weak Goal Chakra: The "Wandering Nomad"

"Where are you going?" "I don't know." "The "Wandering Nomads" are lost and not aligned with how they want to feel toward a desired outcome. Without a clear intention of how one wants to ultimately feel at the end of a project or at the end of the day, one

will become a victim to what others think their Goal should be. How do others know what your outcome should be? The "Wandering Nomad" can be too ambivalent and end up listening to everyone else's opinion instead of themselves. Like a ship without a rudder or direction, one will spend their life following wherever and whatever others think they should go and do and will become continuously disappointed with their personal results and angry at the ones that they listened to.

Manifestation: Indecisiveness

Too Weak Decision Chakra: The "Undecided Vote"

"What do you want to eat?", "I don't care". Or do they? "The "Undecided Voters" have a tough time making decisions and will often go along with the group or another person's opinion to avoid conflict. These people have a need to be liked by others, seek the need for approval, and are too weak to stand up for themselves. These tendencies can be helpful in mediating groups of people and for situations where it's necessary to avoid conflict. However, it is important to stand up for yourself and create what you really want in life and be strong enough to speak your mind and make your own decisions. A trauma that inspires many "Undecided Voters" is if they have had parents who are very angry; a child will always appease the angry parent by not adding anymore conflict and will let the angry one "win." It's time to stand up for yourself and choose what you want in life!

Manifestation: Hungry

Too Weak Director Chakra: "The Mute"

"The Mute" are Too Weak in communicating their feelings in a healthy way. When one has a tough time communicating with others, this can lead to a lot of anger and frustration. These types may have expressed anger before but after a while they find being this way didn't get them what they wanted. Soon people no longer want to work or talk with them. Over time they decided it was better to keep quiet and just bottled up their feelings and ideas as they couldn't communicate in a "nice" way, thus becoming "The Mute".

Manifestation: Hypothyroidism/Hyperthyroidism

Too Weak Connection Chakra: "The Suit of Armor"

When the Connection Chakra is Too Weak, it is difficult for one to communicate their innermost feelings. Our feelings are our way of subconscious communication with one another. If one is limited in communicating their feelings, this person will have little success in maintaining a healthy social network, being a boss where the employees understand them, and frustrated that no one comprehends or listens to what they are saying. For one to be fully empowered in the Connection Chakra, one needs to express their vulnerability. Through our vulnerability we can surrender to asking for help from others. Some think expressing vulnerability is a weakness so instead they will cover it up by creating an energetic "Suit of Armor" around their heart.

Manifestation: Heart Disease

Too Weak Integrity Chakra: "The Sheeple"

The Too Weak Integrity Chakra is the "Wall of the Castle" of the Immune system. This is where rules are held and enforced. However, when one becomes one of "The Sheeple," the rules cannot be enforced thus we get sick, robbed, or cheated on by people. It happens because we take things for granted and assume everything is all right and we do not have to pay attention and become part of "The Sheeple." "The Sheeple" assume that someone else is looking out for them and that if they don't cause a ruckus or ask questions, everything will just remain as is. If we do not keep a keen eye on the rest of the world it may be easy to miss the wolf dressed in sheep's clothing. Strong discernment and paying attention to the details is important in maintaining a healthy immune system and manifesting healthy projects and relationships.

Manifestation: Chronic Sickness

Too Weak Strength Chakra: "The Pushover"

"Just stand up for yourself." The Strength Chakra is the ability of being able to hold things together, like following through on projects or deciding to be happy all day. Strength is like glue or mortar that holds the intentions together that one would like to manifest. If you can stand up for yourself and speak your own mind without bowing down to others, your Strength Chakra will be firm and balanced. However, "The Pushover" cannot do any of this. One may lack strength due to trying to appease angry people and compromising personal integrity by trying to fit in and not rock the boat. These types may have never received healthy validation for their talent and are often just trying to keep the peace by letting the angry ones have their way.

Manifestation: Bad Digestion

Too Weak Passion Chakra: "The Couch Potato"

The Passion Chakra is all about moving forward and action. If one does not have passion for a project or a reason to live, then they are going to go nowhere and accomplish nothing. These people tend to be very mental and have exhausted themselves with either talking or thinking about "it" to death. When it comes time to follow through with completing a task or plan, they are already energetically exhausted and can't physically do anything else. These people would rather be distracted by meaningless time draining activities like watching TV or playing video games, thus the "Couch Potato".

Manifestation: Lethargy, Digestion Issues, Cysts

Too Weak Love Chakra: "The Chastity Belt"

When one has a Too Weak Love Chakra it becomes very hard to physically express one's self which is like wearing a voluntary "Chastity Belt". This category is common among men, as men always need to be macho and cannot express any weakness such as showing how they feel. Many physical male issues that manifest in the lower hip region are due to a lack of expression.

With some people, physical or sexual abuse has happened to them in the past and expressing oneself in a comfortable way is very difficult. Certain cultures that lack physical affection will have a tough time with the thought of greeting others with hugs or kisses on the cheek. People who are not very comfortable dancing may have a weak love chakra due to lack of physical expression.

Manifestation: Bladder, Prostate, Ovarian Cancer

Too Weak Freedom Chakra: "Shipwrecked"

The ability to move and go with the flow is compromised if one is Too Weak in the Freedom Chakra. If one is weak in the Freedom Chakra they will lack the ability to move out of a situation that may not be good for them. They may know that their job is horrible and that it is time to go, but with a weak Freedom Chakra they may spend another 10 years at the dead-end job, till the company closes, they are fired, laid off or share an office with a person that drives them crazy. It may take some extra strength for one who is "Shipwrecked" to gather the courage to sever ties and be able to move on.

Manifestation: Leg Issues, knee/hip/ankle sprains

Your Attraction Pattern affects all aspects of your Life

The "Attraction Pattern" is a phrase that is about which Chakras are Too Strong and Too Weak. When your chakras are out of balance, this creates a polarity that attracts certain circumstances to you. The Universe is always signaling you to stay in balance, so it will give you clues when you are not imbalanced.

Often people will say, "My business life is great, but my personal life is in ruins", and vice versa. However, if one really looks at things, you could identify areas where you think you are doing fine, but you may have the same holes there as well.

I have noticed in sessions with people, that your Attraction Pattern will be imbalanced across all areas of your life in relationships, friends, projects, workplace and your health. The issues will be the same and will constantly point out the holes in your aura. If you make a list of all the troubles, fights, and failures that happen in your life, it is very likely that your "Aura of Attraction Survey" results will capture how things have happened and the same themes of angst repeat themselves. When we can identify this pattern, I believe this is validation for the accuracy of the Survey.

So, in the end if you think you are doing great in business and terrible in your personal life. That may become a short-lived realization. By burying a piece of yourself and putting all your eggs in one basket, one will soon end up with a hole in it. Just focusing on your work will leave a big hole in your personal life. When we can identify your Attractor Pattern then we can focus on the parts of yourself that are not complete yet. When we can repair and strengthen our weakness, and tone down our strengths, we will have a well-rounded life with little to no drama-trauma.

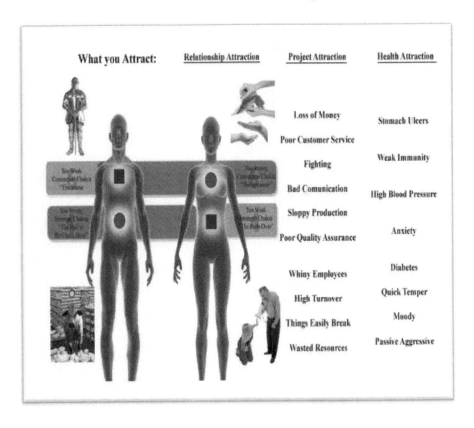

Chapter 4

Cords, Objects, and Entities, oh my!

What are Cords?

The umbilical cord is the closest physical object that we have as an example of a cord. When we are in utero we are corded to our mothers. Through the umbilical cord, we receive nutrients and oxygen from our mother and once it is detached the cording changes into invisible energy cords. Through these invisible cords, we will get support from both of our parents. We are constantly fed energy from our parents until the day we are independent and can fend for ourselves. The "Mother's Intuition" can be described as cording to their child. Once her child is out of the womb, a mother can feel that child through these energetic cords. If the child needs help, the mother will feel it on a certain level, thus the "Mothers' Intuition."

On the left, a mother is connected with a cord to her new baby. On the right, when the child is growing up, invisible energetic cords still support the growing child.

Mental Telepathy

Mental Telepathy works through cords. When we connect to each other or think about each other, we are cording for a moment. How many times have you heard the phone ring or thought of someone and you knew who it was. You just corded to each other. A couple of reasons why mental telepathy does not work is because of the belief that technology does it for us, or we believe it can't be done. But the main reason mental telepathy does not work for some is that it requires listening to one another. Just like operating a walkie-talkie, to hear the other person, one must listen to the other.

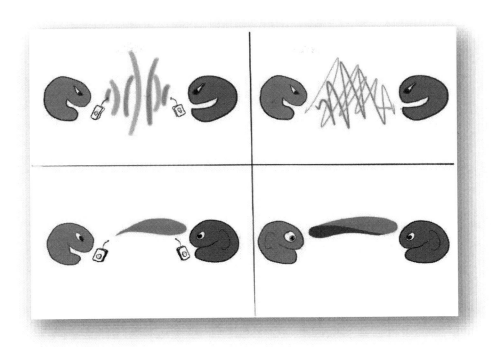

Mental Telepathy requires a person to listen to the other. On the top row, people are talking at the same time and they are frustrated because they cannot communicate. On the bottom row, people are taking turns to listen.

Cords evolve to being Invisible

Over the past decade, we have seen the evolution of cording with technology. The internet and personal computers have shown us that at one time we needed a modem that had a cord to electronically connect to one another. Then we moved to using a router, which became a little faster, and now we are in the age of WIFI (wireless internet). This is a prime example of invisible cords. We saw a cord before and now it is invisible.

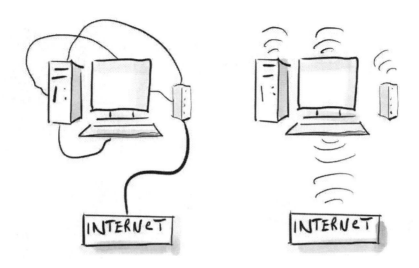

Integrity of Cords

Our energy is dictated by where our mind and focus take us. Our energetic cords are like having infinite arms that feel things for us that are beyond our reach. They could travel around the world, be three feet in front of us or could be right next door. They are feeling out ahead of us and they are always moving, fluctuating, and always guided by where our mind is and what it is doing. What makes them strong is our focus.

If we are distracted, we cannot concentrate our focus and the energy will be weak and scattered. If an archer is about to shoot an arrow at a target, what do they focus on? Do they think about what is for dinner tonight, or what they are going to do this weekend or considering why their friend is mad at them? If the archer is thinking about any of these things, what is the success of their accuracy? Very poor, to say the least. To be successful with each task at hand, we need to be clear and focused and not distracted. Being distracted diffuses our energy which may look like nothing ever gets done.

The same event happens with nutrition. If our bodies are weak from lack of proper nutrients, we will not have the power to hold an intention. Having a strong body will allow the mind to have a stronger focus and attention to complete a desired energetic manifestation. When we are weak, distracted, and in fear, our energetic cords that help us to feel and comprehend the present and future will be compromised.

Why do we cord?

In the beginning of the chapter, we talked about how our parents support and help us energetically through cording. However, if one does not have the benefit of parental cording support or if the parents themselves are not in a healthy balance and cannot support the connection, the child will act out. Most of the time when a young child is acting out it is because the parent has used up all their energy and can't sustain the cording to the child. The child becomes disappointed and feels like they are being ignored and not getting the attention they feel they deserve.

Usually if a child is lacking in a certain area, the parent will kick in with their energy to help fill the gap of the child. Hopefully, through this process the parent is teaching the child to fill their own energetic gap themselves. If this lesson is not taught well and the parent continually does the work for the child, eventually the child will never learn the skills to help themselves. Instead they may learn how to manipulate the parent or as adults, they may manipulate other people to fill their energetic weakness. This scenario tends to turn into extreme dramas that will continually repeat every day for these adult children. When we are out of balance, instead of taking responsibility and filling in our own weakness, we will often play the role of "victim" or tell others "I'm helpless," so that others will hopefully fill in our own imbalance.

As adults, we play these roles because no one taught us we could do it ourselves or we feel that someone else is always going to do things for us.

Helpful Note: If you would like to play the role of empowering yourself, then the first thing to do is to find out what your responsibility is in every aspect of each success or failure. Seeing the patterns of where we continually fail, shows up where we are consistently lacking energy which causes our imbalance. When we can fill this gap ourselves, where we used to see continual failure, we will start to see a new paradigm: Success.

Change the definition of traumas and dramas...instead see them as assets, gifts, and insights for guidance for the future...continually thanking these occurrences is a way to detach from "negative" experiences.

Turning off our Chakra Power

As described earlier, Cords are meant to conduct research for us like antennas on a bee or ant. However, when we start to use them instead to survive, feed off others, and play the victim, we may develop some problems in life.

When we develop a trauma, we may turn a part of ourselves off. We may take this event too personally and think that we alone caused it or that a chakra should be turned off because it is a "bad" chakra. The Universe is always trying to balance us, and it will always lean on our weakest link to make us stronger, just like the wind blowing trees and flowers back and forth. A gentle wind or a severe storm can help make us stronger for future situations by helping us learn to strengthen our roots and branches. The Universe allows us the freedom to lean, bend, and to reach the point of almost breaking on our own so that we may learn the full potential that we have been granted. It is very important to know that we have been given this training ground on Earth to experience the "rules of the Universe." So, we don't need to turn off any chakra and beat ourselves up for energetically stubbing a toe, but instead we could look at how we possibly used this energy wrong and we can try again in another way.

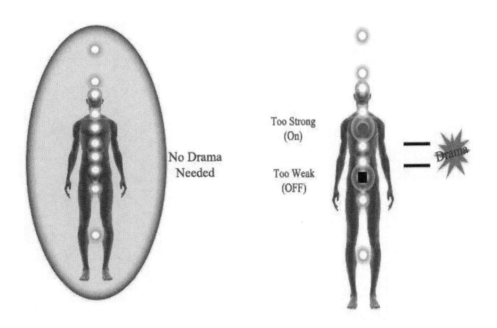

Since we are not perfect yet, we need to recognize when a chakra is turned off or blown out. When a chakra gets turned off it is usually our weakest point in our chakra system. The Universe has pushed on us to make us better, however, we took it personally, and to protect ourselves from any other damage, we turned it off.

We have eternal energy that flows through us like a river down a mountain. However, there is a limit on how much energy we can maintain at once. So, if we turn off a chakra there is potential energy that can go somewhere else. Usually that energy gets transferred to areas that are used the most. Those areas tend to be where we have had our most success. When we receive a trauma and we turn off a part of ourselves, that energy will be transmitted to our greatest strengths. If we are a storyteller, to mask our pain, we will tell more stories and make sure there is never silence so that no one judges us. If we are a comedian, we may always try and be the life of the party, to mask the part of ourselves which has some high insecurity due to not getting enough attention from our busy parents. We may become a judge or an umpire because it is the only way that we will get to have authority since we never had a choice when we were younger from our overbearing parents.

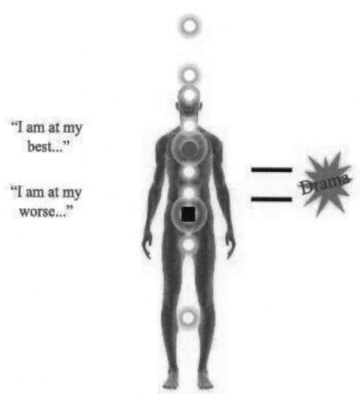

Bigger the Imbalance = Amount of Drama

This is a great defense mechanism in the aura where we can temporarily shut down a part of our selves and have another part take over. However, this is meant to be temporary for a brief time till we can recover and then reboot and turn all our chakras back on. The Universe will give us a break for a bit, but there is a time limit and if we don't turn ourselves back on and read the warning signs, we will be "helped" by the Universe. Usually these helping moments come at a time where they make no sense and we have the feeling of, "why is this happening to me?" In universal time, there is no space and time, so if we turned a part of ourselves off 20 years ago and now we are being pelted by the Universe, we may totally lose the perspective of what the Universe is trying to tell us.

It may seem the Universe does not give us any clues as to what we need to do, if only looking at one event at a time. We need to see the bigger picture of why these things are happening for them to make sense to us. There will be common and repeating clues that happen to us all the time. If one can stop playing the victim by creating dramas with others, they will be able to recognize the repeating messages from the Universe and be able to change and empower their own life.

By going through the Too Strong Too Weak Chapter, one can help themselves figure out precisely where one has turned a part of themselves off. It helps to recognize repeating patterns that happen when you are in a relationship or are creating a project. If one can look at all the points where they failed, one can piece together which chakra is turned off and recognize the pattern that keeps coming up.

One may already know what this area is, which is often the one you are most uncomfortable with and do not want to work on. I challenge you to take it on and become strong in your weakness. If one can take a step back emotionally so as not to take it too personally, one can see how they turned off the chakra in the first place. When one can take out the personal offensiveness and just calmly observe it as a learning experience, then the chakra will turn back on.

When we turn a chakra back on, it will give relief to the chakra that has been too strong. This is how we burn out our talents, by always using them to carry the load of all the other chakras that are turned off. Most people are running on two to five of the 10 chakras. This is too exhausting and is like walking everywhere on one foot and wondering why your foot hurts and why it takes you so long to get anywhere. When we use our talents to make up for what we are lacking, we will burn out with the things we love, the jobs we

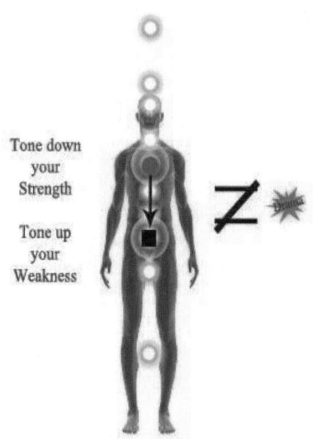

Bigger the Imbalance = Amount of Drama

had passion for, and the love of life we deserve. Balance is the key in strengthening our weaknesses and toning down our strengths.

Opposites Attract? Sort of…

Why do I keep dating the same jerks?

When we are in a friendship, family, or work environment the quality of the relationship will reflect what we attract. If you are Too Weak in the Heart Connection Chakra you will attract someone else that is equally Too Strong in that same chakra. In most relationships, we are bartering and trading each other's energy. "I'll trade you some heart energy for some of your strength energy."

We may think we choose people by their looks or their bank account. However, the first thing we do when choosing our next mate is to pick someone who counters our own chakra system. Subconsciously, we will choose someone by the bartering system of "you complete me," which really means, "I have what you need, and you have what I need equally. Then the next category after energy matching will be by looks and then perhaps bank account.

The best and healthy relationship is a balance of no more than a 40-60% relationship. For example, if one person in a relationship is using 40% of their heart, they will attract someone who is 60% strong in the heart, which will add up to 100%. Ideally, we want to be using our chakras to be energetically 50% which will attract a partner that is equally using 50%. If we have a Too Strong Chakra our energy output will be 60-90% and when we have a Too Weak Chakra our energy output will be 10-40%. Being Too Strong or Too Weak will equate to an unending drama-fest in a relationship. The goal of this book is to make you aware of your own drama and so that you can correct it yourself and become more balanced.

The "jerks" you attract will be in the extreme ranges of the chakra system, which ultimately reflects on you, because that is who you are attracting. If you can help identify where you specifically attract these "jerks" in your energetic aura, then you can change who comes near you. After energy balancing and healing have taken place, you may never attract another "jerk."

The "Aura of Attraction Survey" in the Too Strong Too Weak Chapter can help you determine your own percentages.

How we really choose our Relationships

The next illustration is an example of how our energy can be matched with another. This is how we first match up with people. I think this will also explain how we have witnessed relationships and asked ourselves, "How do those two go together?"

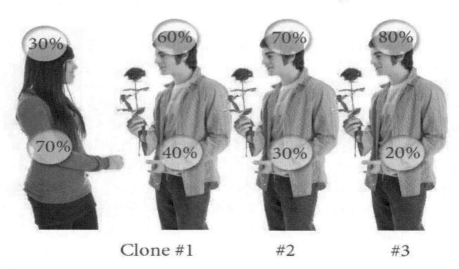

In the illustration, the lady has her own energy pattern. On the right are our three clones, but they all have different energy patterns. Who does she pick?

The answer is the #2 Clone. In this illustration, the lady is 30% in the upper chakras and has a 70% energetic output in the lower chakras. The man is her opposite. They both will enjoy each other for a bit, but in a 70-30% match there will be some drama and hopefully they will figure things out to get to a 40-60% relationship which is more peaceful.

Energetic Match with Clone #2

The Loudest Gets the Blame

Often the loud and angry person will get the credit for ruining the relationship. However, the silent, unemotional victim is equally the problem. The loud angry one must yell because the silent one is often passive and does nothing. Characteristics of being too loud and overly angry are usually coming from a Too Strong Chakra. The silent partner is usually the result of having a Too Weak Chakra. If the silent one would strengthen their voice, the angry one wouldn't have to yell at all. But as attractor patterns go, if the angry one was balanced with their anger they would have never attracted the silent one in the first place. If a person falls into the category of extreme drama and has a chakra of 10% but could strengthen that chakra to at least 40% and they would notice the drama in their next relationship to be considerably less. Both people in a relationship need to acknowledge their own half of each drama and take ownership of it.

The Too Strong Too Weak Chakra model can also be used when looking at the Western Medical system. Typically, the Too Strong or "loudest" set of symptoms usually gets the greatest attention, and the Too Weak symptoms are often ignored. This is also where Western Medicine has failed with every sickness or disease because there are always two parts to every illness. For every illness, there will be part of the body that is Too Strong and another that is Too Weak. Both must be addressed, however, usually the Too Strong issue will be the only part that is examined. The Too Strong organ must work harder because the Too Weak non-performing organ is not working. In Western Medicine only one of the two are treated. There is an imbalance and if the treatment does not work to reach balance then you will have a chronic-never-resolving health issue.

Attachment & Detachment of Cords

Know when to hold them and when to fold them

A misuse of your energy or cords can lead to many of the dramas and diseases of today. This next story illustrates when to detach cords from another or what happens when one does not detach them.

"The Fallen Man on the Sidewalk"

The figure on the Left gives the "fallen person" Connection (6) and Strength (4) energy to help them stand up.

It is a nice summer day and you go out to your favorite park to get some exercise. As you are walking you notice that someone has fallen in front you. You help this person up.

Energetically there are two ways that this will end regarding cording. You will either attach to someone with energetic cords permanently or you will attach to them temporarily. When you help someone up physically you are giving your energy away to the fallen one. Energy and cords are filling in the gaps that the fallen person needs to help them stand up again and regain their balance.

Once the fallen person stands up again we ask, "Are you Okay?" When it is confirmed that they are all right and the fallen man has thanked the person for helping them up…. then the cord is Cut! Once the cords are cut we bring the energy back to ourselves. This is an example of healthy cording and detachment.

The other way this scenario can end up is with a person who cannot detach from this trauma. They will go home and still worry about the person who has fallen, and they can't stop wondering if they are alright. They may have gotten the fallen person's phone number and gave them some money. Some would look at this scenario and think that the worried person is being nice.

But worrying about everything in the world and all the things that are out of your control, including the fallen person, is futile. All anyone can do is inspire and guide others. When we get caught up in feeling as if we must take care of every detail and we take responsibility for everything and others, we will end up with no energy for ourselves and will have no time to live our lives.

When we help people, we use our empathy to feel how others are doing through our Heart which is the Connection Chakra. When this Chakra is balanced, it is easy to detach from someone. However, for those who have a Connection Chakra that is Too Strong, it may be very hard for this person to detach and will not feel content until the "fallen person" takes all their energy from them. We need to trust that others need to learn their own lessons and it is not our responsibility to learn it for them. Otherwise, one will get their own lesson on how they should not give all their energy away to others, if they still need to learn that principal.

Healthy energetic cord detachment. Energy was shared between these two people and when they leave each other, they will keep their own energy

Too Strong Connection Chakra cannot detach from the fallen person. They are still worried about them. Thus, cords are still in place and energy is being wasted.

Scenarios of Learning to Cord

Learned Behavior and Survival

There are two major ways we cord: Learned Behavior and Survival. Most of the imbalances that we accumulate were initiated between the ages of 0-5 years old. The reasons they follow us to adulthood are because these lessons were the first ones we learned, and this is where a lot of our memory was first being developed but because we were so young we do not remember a lot of the circumstances that happened to us. We forget that as children we turned a part of ourselves off as a protection mechanism, so when we become adults we need to learn how to turn our power back on.

Behavioral Learning

"Turn your anger on just like mommy"

Learned behavior cording happens when we watch our parent's behavior or the people around us. Our parents will have their own imbalances and usually we will copy one parent or characteristics of both. Just like we learn to eat with a fork and how to talk, we will also learn how to turn our heart off and speak with anger.

Learned Behavior: "Green Child" observes their parent manipulate the energy of another adult. On right, child manipulates a friend just like the parent did.

If a child is learning how to live and act in society, they are also naturally going to use their energy in the same way as a parent who is angry. If a parent has their Strength Chakra on Too Strong, their child is going to copy this energy and act the same way. If a parent is manipulative, the child will use these learned skills to also get what they want. The child will think this is perfectly normal as they will see the benefits of taking advantage of others and its "effectiveness".

Survival Learning

"Turn your throat off, so the monster doesn't get you."

As a child, we come into the world with innocence. We think the world is full of unicorns and gumdrops. We do not know about anger, depression, and danger. As a child when these things happen to us we have no idea how to deal with them or understand what has occurred. When we are exposed to these negative events or people, we tend to shut things down to protect ourselves and our innocent nature.

A very common issue I have dealt with in my practice is the "Loud Child" who has throat or thyroid issues as an adult. At the age of around 2-3 we are busy using our voices and seeing what comes out of them. However, if there is a parent around that is normally angry or does not know how to communicate well with a "Loud Child", the parent may discipline a child to be quiet by yelling at them or using physical abuse. Quick words like "shut up" may be applied. This behavior surprises the child because the child has no idea what "shut up" means or the simple fact that they don't even know what "too loud" means. All the child understands is that their presence is making the parent mad. They don't know what to do other than not make a sound. So, the child will turn off their throat chakra to protect themselves from upsetting the parent and to protect themselves from being randomly screamed at. If a child has grown up with these issues, once they become an adult, thyroid issues may have manifested, or they may have the inability to express what they need from others.

With regression therapy, by determining when an issue initially occurred, we can change the outcomes of our lives. We do not have to accept "this is the way we are" and can transform and evolve from any situation.

The Science of Epigenetics states that our genes can be changed by our attitude, nutrition, and mental behavior. We are not a victim to our genes. I like to think of genes like a used car that gets passed down through the generations. Once you get your "car" handed down you may have squeaky breaks, a broken tail light, and a kicked in fender. However, there are auto body shops and you can get all those things, fixed just like what counseling, massage, or nutrition can do for your body and overall health.

"There is no such thing as a genetic disease, every disease is due to a Nutritional Deficiency."

Dr. Joel Wallach, ND

Epigenetics: The Death of the Genetic Theory of Disease Transmission

Objects

Objects are thought forms that can manifest into energetic material that can influence others. They can be used to take energy from others, sabotage a specific area of the body, or are used to punish and hurt another individual. Having an object in one's body is the same idea as having a stick lodged in the spokes of a bicycle. Our energy is spiraling like a wheel and if you want to turn the wheel off, you can create a form of energy to stop it. An object will compromise a person's energy system and will cause an energy disturbance that may affect their health, social issues, and success with projects. In Medical Intuitive sessions with clients, I have been able to see these objects and they will appear as metaphors that help tell the story of how things happen. I see knives and weapons from those that want to hurt people. I have seen satellite dishes and software devices in those who want to control others. I can see who placed these objects there and why. When I pull these objects out I can feel the weight of it in my hands, which feels like a ball of plasma. Other sensitive people can see and feel the objects in my hands. I like to play a game of which hand is holding the plasma ball, surprising a lot of people guess correctly.

Where objects land

Objects will be in the form of how they are intended, such as a "Knife in the back." Yes, I have pulled many knives out of the backs of people. This really happens! Usually this is a result of jealousy issues between one person and another. The recipient of the knife will have no idea that this person they trusted would or could do such a thing to them. The middle of the back is a very vulnerable position in the body and cannot be defended easily. It is a prime location to hit someone energetically and they will have no idea what hit them.

The placement of where an object lands depends on the intention of the attacker and the ignorance or innocence of the victim. When an object is implanted in the front of our body, the attacker wants to make sure that they get credit for the attack.

If an object is attached on the side, then a person didn't mean to attack another, and they just couldn't help themselves and didn't know what they were doing.

If the object is in the back, then the person really wanted to hurt them but didn't want the victim to know who their attacker was.

Objects will stick to you if you allow them to stay. That is right victims! It is just as much as your fault that the object sticks to you as the person that stuck you with them. Objects can stick by appeasing the bully to allow continually taking of your lunch money or by wanting to be ignorant to situations and by being naïve and assuming that, "They would never do that, they are so nice". Often a person is in denial and does not see the reality of a situation.

The more I work with objects the more I know that they are real. As a Medical Intuitive we are dealing with a lot of invisible objects. It is very hard to prove if any of this is true, however, if you convey to your client what you are seeing then they often will agree and can even feel the objects being removed. At this moment in time I am convinced that the images I see are very real. Some people have so many objects in them that it is a good thing that objects are invisible or else they wouldn't be able to walk through a door.

Self-Sabotage with Objects: *"Oh good, now I have an excuse!"*

The same areas of implanting objects in the front, side, or back also work with one who sabotages themselves. When we turn off a chakra we may create an object to help compromise our energy, like the "wrench thrown in the machine". We instead use our mind to blame that wrench for our problems instead of taking personal responsibility for ourselves causing the problem.

A common issue of self-sabotage I see is with those who injure their feet. The legs are ruled by the Freedom Chakra and the Bladder Meridian. This issue is about the "ability to let things go". People who break their toes or continuously trip are trying to sabotage themselves from not having to decide. So, if one continually hurts their feet which gives them the freedom to move about, they get to have the excuse of, "Oh well, I hurt my foot, now I don't have to make that choice." The excuse is now created, and they can continue to be indecisive.

I have also seen someone who did not want to initiate a decision; they were Too Strong in the Freedom Chakra and Too Weak in the Strength Chakra. This led them to have "concrete boots" in the etheric level. In their aura, their energy was trapped below their ankles, giving them a pain in their calf. They knew that they had to decide but due to the excuse of self-inflicting energetic concrete boots and having a Too Weak Strength Chakra buy they did not have the strength to lift the boots, thus the self-creation of the convenience of making a sabotaging decision instead of making a proactive helpful one.

Skewered in the Back

"Will it also make you happy if I stab myself as well?"

One of my clients suffered from chronic back pain. She revealed to me that she is an "out-of-the-closet lesbian" and her family was not happy about it at all.

Upon using my intuitive vision to see these objects I could feel and see objects piercing through her back and coming out of her front. Before I remove an object, I like to know why it is in the region and who initiated the attack. Also, it is important to know why the person initiated the attack and why the victim allowed themselves to be attacked. Once this is known and relayed to the client then it is easier to remove, and the healing can take place quicker.

I saw two objects in this woman - a sword and a bamboo staff. The sword was from her family and they were very upset with her and did not approve of this gay behavior. The bamboo staff was self-inflicted from the guilt of her choice and the disappointment she had brought to her family.

It had been a couple of years since this "out of the closet" moment so she had come to terms with these issues and she was ready to heal them. The handle of the sword and bamboo staff where located on her back, so this meant the objects entered through her back. This also meant her family was very mad at her but did not know that these negative feelings have consequences. We hold on to these objects for people because we think by holding on to them we are agreeing with those people. We incorrectly believe that this would make them accept us because we are taking their punishment.

I removed both objects. The sword came out very cleanly, but the bamboo staff was a little bumpier and harder to remove. Afterward we talked, and she noticed which object was being taken out. She could feel the sword easily pulled out and with the bamboo staff she felt the knobs of the bamboo as it was being extracted.

This was a confirming story that these images were not just my imagination but that these objects are real, and I have also worked with other people where we see the same objects together.

Stabbed in the Front

"I want to marry your son, what can I do to hurt myself for you?"

I met a lady, named Brea, and she was complaining of chest pains that she felt every time she was around her soon to be Mother-in-Law. The Mother did not approve of Brea and every time Brea was around her she started having chest pains. Brea speculated that the Mother-in-Law did not approve of the future marriage.

I began to look at the energetics of Brea's heart. There was a series of small knives lodged in her heart. I could feel it was from the Mother-in-Law and that the message was, "I do not approve of you, you are not good enough for my son and you make me so mad that I want to let you know that I am causing you this pain."

This is an example of objects that enter through the front. These people are not hiding anything and are very willing to let the other know of their disgust for the them.

Mother-in-Law energetically stabs soon to be Daughter-in-Law with Director Chakra (7).
She forcefully stabs Brea in the heart. Open hearted Brea (Too Strong Connection Charka (6) takes the hit hoping to appease the Mother-in-Law. (Circled numbers represent Too Strong Chakras, Squared numbers represent Too Weak Chakras.)

Brea already knew she wanted to be accepted by the Mother-in-Law, so she was ready to appease her to be liked. An object can easily attach to someone if they let down their guard for another to step on them. Brea opened her heart and let the Mother-in-Law take a shot at her; Brea thought that this appeasement would make the Mother happy.

What may be better is to stand up to the Mother and not let the shot happen in the first place. Perhaps this may earn some respect from the Mother instead of being a victim. One may be better off by knowing someone may not like you, rather than living with recurrent chest pains.

"No one can make you feel inferior without your consent."

— Eleanor Roosevelt, *"This is My Story"*

Stabbed in the Side

"Good-bye everyone, I'm off to College,

Anyone want to stab me before I go?"

Jill came to my office complaining of severe abdominal pains. Upon "seeing" her side, it looked like she had been hit with a "trailer hitch". It just looked like a brutal hunk of metal lodged in her side. I could trace the image of the "hitch" and that was the area of the pain.

When Jill was 19 years old and she was heading off to college and leaving the family nest for the first time. Jill also has a younger sister and the two were as close as sisters can be. I have seen this many times when the oldest child goes off to college. The younger siblings were very sad to see their older siblings leave and they lashed out at the older ones.

The younger sister lashed out at Jill because she didn't want her to leave and wanted her to stay. With her intention, she attacked her older sister in the side. When one is attacked in the side it means that the attacker didn't really mean to hurt the other. Jill was vulnerable to attack because she felt guilty for leaving her younger sister. This left Jill open for the younger sister to vent her issues and Jill thought, "Well if you hit me will that make you feel better?"

This event happened 20 years ago, and the lingering unresolved issues accumulated into a debilitating issue. Time does not necessarily heal all wounds.

All pain must be balanced, or it will linger forever.

Entities

Entities are interdimensional beings that are invisible, and we cannot see. They are ghosts, demons, disembodied souls, and people who have died but have not entered the light and are still roaming around.

Entities follow the same rules of cording as previously mentioned at the beginning of the chapter. They are still hanging around because they are still continually cording off other people. They may "haunt" a house because they cannot let go of the memory of the place that may still give them energy.

Entities will attach themselves to people in the same way that they did when they were living. They will be attracted to those who possess their energetic match. A living person will attract entities if they do not have strong boundaries themselves. Entities are a little tough to defend because they are invisible.

Usually when we are at our lowest or in extreme distress, it is because our chakras have reached an extreme imbalance. We may ask for help but if one is not specific with the call for help, that leaves the door open for anything to come in.

One may pray for help because they have depleted their heart, which to them means they need heart support. An entity can hear this and they can come over and fill the void. Their energetic imbalance may appear to match the person in distress. The one in distress welcomes the company and now the two are in union like a parasite and its host.

For survival sake and for a limited time this may be alright. One may feel the entities and their voices because now they are joined in a relationship and they may have a common agenda.

After a time, the one in distress may start to feel better and would like to move on. However, when one has an entity attached it may be hard to change the imbalance on their own. When a person desires balance, this will start to shake apart the previous agreement with the entity and the energetic agreement will be broken. It may be tough for the once distressed person to move on because the entity will whisper in the person's ear not to change, "I can't protect you anymore, what about me, I'll die if you let me go?" At one time, this agreement may have been helpful for survival, but now it is time for the person to be strong and move on because they need to have their own integrity and stand upon their own feet for true balance.

Entities will attach to your weakness. Person on the right is Too Weak in the Goal Chakra (9) and Connection Chakra (6).

People who have auras that are thick, dark, gloomy, slimy, or are "energetic vampires" may have a whole host of entities. It is like having a fighting family attached to them all the time. These people may be hard to talk to or it may be difficult to reason with them. They must consult all those entities at once for all of them to move together. The collective agreement to host all these entities will be centered around taking from others. The host can only supply so much energy to support the entities, so they begin manipulating others and take their energy.

People who are overly generous with their energy may fall victim to entities. If you are leaking out energy and lack integrity to put boundaries around your energy reserves, it is just like putting blood in the water where sharks will find you. Being generous is not bad, it becomes bad when we do not monitor ourselves and give away more than we receive.

Alcoholics are prime examples of those that can be taken over by entities. When an alcoholic passes out from excessive drinking, this leaves the person wide open for entity attachments. It is like no one is tending the store and people are looting all the products. An alcoholic is pretty much saying, "I can't do this anymore; someone else take over." This occurs when the alcoholic is not monitoring their energy and lets it leak out; the entities are free to lap it up and become attached to the host. With alcoholics, you can see the look in their eyes that "no one is home, just us monsters". The heavy empty feelings are the entities overwhelming the person and when they attract so many, it becomes difficult to get them off. They prefer the alcoholic to be in peril as this will release more energy for the entities to absorb.

To help an alcoholic, it is important to detox them and once that has begun, then they need to address their emotional issues and fill in the imbalance of their chakras. We need to become strong where we are weak, and this will make us invincible to any situation that we put ourselves in.

The main purpose of this book is to repeat often that there is a limit to our energy and that we need to protect every drop of it: we guide and inspire others by being an example of how to be balanced so others have a model that they can copy for themselves.

"Be the change that you wish to see in the world."

— *Mahatma Gandhi*

Praying

Praying does not have to be restricted or solely reserved for those who consider themselves to be religious. Consider praying to be another form of thinking like wishing, having good intentions or practicing positive affirmations.

In our world, we have free will. Nothing has power over you unless you let it. Even if someone is positively praying for you, if you are the one receiving someone's prayer, you should want the help. Otherwise nothing will happen to you.

The way one fashions a prayer together is very important. If you are praying for someone and you want a specific outcome, it is likely the intention will not happen. Often people get into trouble because they are trying to learn a specific lesson and if you try and step in and pray that their issue will go away the prayer is likely to have no effect. To keep their free will intact and for your prayer to be effective, try out this prayer. "May they move

toward their own healing., I pray that they will ask for help, or I pray that they will live their original intention." This technique also opens things up the possibility to allow the Universe to step in as well. Sometimes if we allow the Universe to step in and help, usually a better result will occur than our original plea. For this reason, letting go of specific expectations is important. Another flaw in praying is constantly worrying about someone. This is a negative form of praying and it is like a continual form of affirming that the person needing the prayers cannot do it themselves. This is where one can constantly cord to another and negatively affirm to the person that they cannot be helped. The person praying is also not letting the person they are praying for be free, rather they are keeping them in a holding pattern. When we do not let go of worry, the prayer is not being sent to the person we are praying for. To make a prayer intention successful it must be positive and when you send it out, you must fully let go of it and completely forget about it. This also affirms with confidence that your prayer is going to happen, so don't worry about it. Worrying about the prayer cancels the original positive prayer. Worrying is an affirmation that prayer does not work. So, stay positive and trust that the Universe is working with you. Sometimes some people need harder lessons than others and you need to trust that their soul has their own free will.

Energy Vampires

Vampires have been quite popular recently due to their sexiness, immortality, and super powers. This also leads to people fantasizing about wanting to meet them or be them. I do not know if vampires really exist, but I do believe if any type of lore can last the test of time there must be some truth to it.

The context of this passage is related to the nature of vampirism and how they need to take something from someone else for their own gain. There are a group of people who label themselves as Energy Vampires and they think they are in some way like the Vampires of lore that drink blood. They believe that to survive, they need to take energy from others. These people like to think they are being ethical in getting permission from donors and this type of validation is acceptable.

In business, these people are usually selling something that is outdated, doesn't work, or is a fraud. They usually will try and manipulate and swindle people into buying their scams because they know that what they are selling doesn't work. For them it is all about making money for themselves with little thought for helping others.

Have you ever talked with a family member or friend who constantly gets themselves into drama-filled situations and then they want to dump it on you? This is their way of not being responsible for their actions and passing their horrible drama on to another. After you get empathetic and listen to their story you may feel drained, because you played the victim and gave them energy. This can be rightly called energy vampirism; even if it is subconscious they are taking someone else's energy.

These self-proclaimed energy vampires are also taking other's energy but on a very conscious level. If one was to consider their past, one may find that one or both parents were alcoholics, overbearing, physical or verbally abusive. These types of characteristics would be taking energy from the child and the child would soon learn that they cannot store energy themselves as it is quickly taken. The child would build a defense mechanism around them and it would be tough growing into adulthood with healthy boundaries. As adults, they feel it is natural and normal to steal other's energy as it was so often stolen from them.

Cord cutting

Cord cutting is a technique that is used by many healers. There is still a lot of uncertainty about this subject among the energetic healer community. I have heard everything from, "cutting cords is bad and never should be done", to "all cords are unnecessary it doesn't matter if they are cut". I believe the middle is true and that cutting cords should not be done by amateurs and in my view, there is a lot to it and it is an advanced technique.

The cord cutting technique that I use comes a lot from the knowledge in this chapter. We must learn how our dramas are manifested and claim responsibility for our actions, so we can learn from them. We must strengthen our weaknesses and tone down our strengths, so we do not weaken our passions. This must be understood first before we go and cut cords. We need to establish a firm foundation of rules and then we need to guide the one whose cord has been cut to what balance is. If we cut the cords and the person does not know what balance is, then the cords will shortly reattach again in the same manner as before. It will seem like something happens for a day or so, but if that person does not know what their balance is to them, they will be back in your office again or think that the healer and the technique are ineffective.

In the example of the "man who fell on the sidewalk" we saw an instance of self-cord cutting. The helper saw that when the fallen person got help standing back up and then saw that they were fine, the helper was able to cut their own helping cords. So, it is possible to help ourselves and to cut your own cords by using self-reflection or asking for penance or forgiveness.

Albert Einstein said, "We can't solve problems by using the same kind of thinking we used when we created them." So, with larger life-long issues of cord cutting, sometimes it is harder to figure something out yourself with the same mindset that created the situations. Asking for help from a therapist or energetic healer gives one the third-party view of your situation. A third party is unbiased and does not have the same emotional attachments than the one who needs their cords cut. Success can come a lot more quickly and easier with some support and tough love from another.

My technique of cord cutting has evolved through the years and now I am at a point where I have settled into a system that I have found to be safe, effective, and long lasting. I used to identify every cord, object, and entity in a session but now I only need to balance the chakras. When imbalanced chakras are leveled, the cords, objects, and entities that were in the imbalance will disappear because now there is nowhere for them to attach. Of course, the success of proper balancing is to ask the following question: Did one get all the way to the core issue that caused the whole imbalance in the first place? If not, then the balance would not work, and we just need to keep working at it until the balance can hold. Sometimes it takes a few sessions as we can only integrate so much information at once. We cannot expect to get everything solved in one or two sessions for issues that have been validated for a lifetime. It takes a while and some patience is necessary to see the full process through, but it is well worth finding the underlying cause of the issue so that is will not recur.

Early in my Medical Intuitive career I found I can detach cords and remove objects from people very easily. However, I had yet to learn how to work with the Universe. I was busy trying to hold on to everyone's objects that I pulled out and solved everything myself. This led to sleepless nights of insomnia and grinding my teeth. Finally, I did a meditation on it and asked my Higher Self/ Angels what to do. They said, "Pass the objects from your clients to us, that is our job. Your job is to only point them out. It takes a lifetime to change negative objects back into objects of light and you don't have time for that." This came as a great relief to know that I don't have to do everything and there is help if we ask for it.

An object is taken out of the client. The object is then thrown into the one-way Angel Realm

When cutting the cords of a client, I now ask for help from the Angels to help heal the other person that the client is attached to. This is like a prayer where I'm asking for a higher power to step in and assist another's healing.

For object dispersal, I envisioned a portal or door that is a one-way door to the Angels and I pass all negative things to them. I make sure to close the door since it is just like a garbage can where I place the object in and forget about it. When it is there it is not coming back. Detach from it. Cut the energy cord.

After a balancing, the issue is done and resolved. It only comes back if the person still wants to continue the drama. They will then become imbalanced and a new object will come to take up the space and will attach to them again. In session, I try and make it very clear how imbalances happen so the person does not repeat the imbalance and the object will never re-attach.

Questionable Cord Cutting Techniques

I was once involved in an organization that liked to help people. However, what I really saw them doing was creating drama so then they could clean it up, much like what I see with Politicians. It made them feel important, but they did have good intentions and I believe they were a little misguided.

Their cord cutting technique involved a knife and incense. At the time, I liked the technique because of the ceremony around it, but I soon dropped it from my repertoire because it did not have a long-lasting effect and taught no healing lesson to anybody.

They would take a knife and use it to draw a circle around the person whose cords were going to be cut. A stick of incense was used to represent the trapped residue of the cords. Once the incense was burned out, that meant the cording issue was over and the ceremony was complete.

I think this technique is great for someone who wanted a general energetic clearing. Sometimes when we are in "dirty" places or we have been energetically attacked by others we may have clouds of bad energy on us, much like being in a fight where we get bruises and scrapes. But as for cord cutting in a healthy way, I do not think this technique helps. It may help someone if they are very aware of themselves and their energy when the cords are cut. Then that person can put the cords back themselves in a healthy way. If one does not know what this means, then have someone else help you.

When we have our cords cut, we were attached to someone else and we are breaking the previous agreement with that person. That other person may want to reattach to the original person. When a person has their cords cut to help the other person who is being detached from, they need to be sent angels and prayers to help them to become a temporary surrogate of the cords. Otherwise, that person may track them down and start some drama, so they can reattach. Often during a cord cutting, hours later or during that moment in session, the other person who is on the end of being detached with will call the cutee. I instruct people to not use the phone for a few days and let the new energetic alignment settle.

That is why it is important to know where we are weak so that we can strengthen this area and be aware when people try to do the same technique that tricked us or took advantage of us. After a cord cutting we are a bit vulnerable afterward. The Universe will test us again by asking, "Are you sure you want to go that way?" Therefore, I want to highlight what things look like in a balanced state so when we are tested we can make a new decision and stay there with conviction. This is what healing really is: Learning the lessons and ways of the Universe on our own terms and in our own way.

Cord cutting can be effective in removing emotional cords between people and entities, however, objects seem to be a little more embedded into the energetic body, which may require a technique called etheric surgery or object extraction. This technique requires a little more skill to be able to handle the objects, hold the energy of the person and then sew the energy up properly. Objects need to be removed for chakra balancing. Objects have their own weight and they can tip the scale of a person's energetic imbalance.

If not done correctly and the "wound" is not taken care of properly, the client can become sick as the "wound" can cause an energetic "infection".

On left: Client and Healer (cord cutter) On Right: Angel and the one whose cording is being cut away from client. Angel helps this person resolve and heal

(Please ask someone how to do the afore-mentioned techniques, since these are advanced techniques and do require some training. I have also left out some key information as well. Improper technique can make yourself and/or make your clients sick.)

Continue the greatness with:

"The Aura of Attraction"

Become Healthier, Wealthier, and Wiser

By Being Aware of

What You Attract

Vol 2

On the Amazon Bookstore

Topics include….

- ✓ Energetic Balancing at the workplace
- ✓ How to hire
- ✓ Leadership
- ✓ Playing competitive sports and keeping your soul.
- ✓ Nature says yes only man says no
- ✓ How to study
- ✓ How does WAR start
- ✓ Answer to Cancer – energetically
- ✓ Incurable Disease – or have we just skipped something?
- ✓ Self-Practices – How to reach your soul's purpose, how to meditate, how to pray,
- ✓ Examples of Relationship scenario how we fit together.

Take the Aura of Attraction Quiz in the App located on Jacob Caldwell's Facebook Fanpage at

https://www.facebook.com/TheAuraofAttraction/

or

www.JacobCaldwell.com

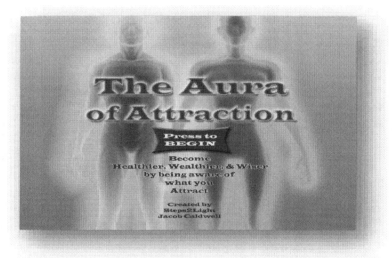

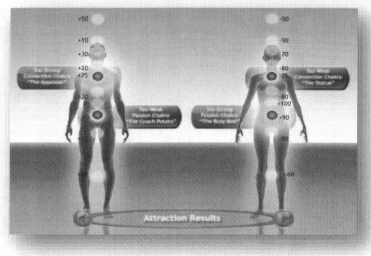

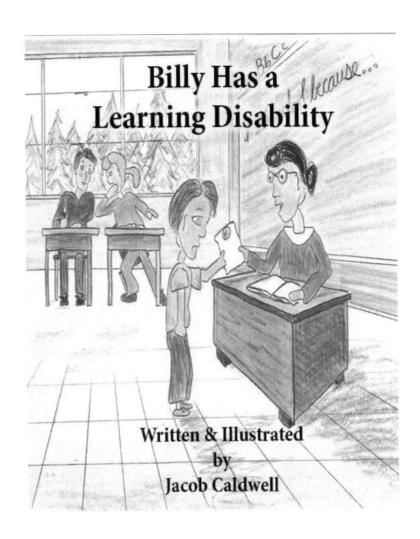

Billy is a boy who has just been told he has a Learning Disability. Billy and his mother work with a tutor who helps him discover that he doesn't have a disability, just that he things differently and has no disability at all. The tutor and Billy work on special tasks that help Billy realize his own Learning Skills.

Jacob was inspired to write this book about the way people walked around and interacted with other or not. It almost seemed like they wanted to disappear. Well, what if they could?

In this story an Inventor creates a Plastic Suit Bubble that people can use to shield themselves from all the things they fear. In the end, perhaps the bubble is more trouble than people can fubble.

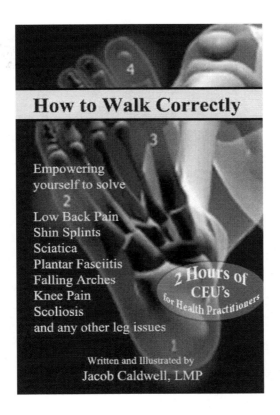

This guide on How to Walk Correctly is for people who want to be responsible for their own healing. This step by step process of walking correctly will help you alleviate your own leg issues. This is one of the ways to never have to be in a wheel chair or the need to wear orthotics. Walking Correctly will help your overall posture and many of your leg, back, and neck chronic issues may be able to lessen or disappear.

Jacob Caldwell is a Massage Therapist in Seattle who will assist you in empowering you to heal yourself. He has over 15 years of experience in helping people see that you can alleviate your own symptoms by just Walking Correctly.

Dr. Joel Wallach's - Essential 90 Pak

The basic daily pak for everyday health. Get your 90 Essential Vitamins and Minerals for your health.

Beyond Tangy Tangerine 2.0 Citrus Peach Fusion® - 480g canister

This advanced multi-vitamin mineral complex is formulated with probiotics and all the 90 essential vitamins and minerals

Ultimate EFA Plus™- 90 soft gels

Good for the brain, heart and more, this blend of essential fatty acids (i.e. Omega's) is derived from flax seed oil, fish oil, and borage oils.

Beyond Osteo-fx™ powder - 357g Canister

Optimal for bone and joint health, this contains nutrients that enhance calcium and magnesium absorption in an easy to consume powder form.

BUY WHOLESALE HERE

http://nutrihealing.my90forlife.com/

http://steps2light.my90forlife.com/

Description of The Aura of Attraction

The Aura of Attraction is the collection of illustrated observations from the viewpoint of Medical Intuitive, Jacob Caldwell. He is the author and illustrator of this book. A Medical Intuitive can read people's energy and this book is an illustration on what he has been able to observe. He has been able to turn the invisible visible and demonstrate that the clues of life's guidance are within us. Jacob will help you interpret the daily signs that you receive ad help to find the answers to questions you keep asking. He has been able to see how people create their own disease, circumstances, and good or bad relationships. He has created a book that will help those that want to take the reins of their life and change it for the better. If you are tired of riding the same daily merry-go-round of insanity and you want to get off, then pick up this book and get ready to step out into your true empowerment. Set your life on your terms and fill it with new meaning by being able to interpret the clues that are all around you, to create a happy life.

Check out Jacob's other Web Sites

Join the Members Only club
for healings, questions,
and personal Medical Intuitive Sessions.
Thanks!

Email: steps2light@yahoo.com
www.SeattleMassageBlogger.com
www.SeattleMassage.co
www.EnergyHealingTherapy.net
www.JacobCaldwell.com